GOD'S MAN

The Story of Pastor Niemoeller

Martin and Else Niemoeller
on a recent visit to the United States

GOD'S MAN

THE STORY OF PASTOR NIEMOELLER

By Clarissa Start Davidson

GREENWOOD PRESS, PUBLISHERS
WESTPORT, CONNECTICUT

Library of Congress Cataloging in Publication Data

Davidson, Clarissa Start.
  God's man.

    Reprint of the ed. published by I. Washburn,
New York.
    Bibliography: p.
    1. Niemoller, Martin, 1892-   2. Lutheran
Church--Clergy--Biography. 3. Clergy--Germany, West--
Biography. I. Title.
[BX8080.N48D3 1979]   284'.1'0924 [B]   78-10131
ISBN 0-313-21065-9

Copyright © 1959 by Clarissa Start Davidson

Reprinted with the permission of David McKay Company, Inc.

Reprinted in 1979 by Greenwood Press, Inc.
51 Riverside Avenue, Westport, CT 06880

Printed in the United States of America

10 9 8 7 6 5 4 3 2 1

ACKNOWLEDGMENTS

I am grateful to Colonel Richard H. Stevens for permission to quote him extensively and to the *Sunday Express,* London, for permission to quote his account; to *The Christian Century* for permission to quote from their publication; and to G. P. Putnam's Sons for permission to quote from *Austrian Requiem* by Kurt von Schuschnigg (copyright 1946 by G. P. Putnam's Sons).

C. S. D.

FOREWORD

WHEN I was a college student we prayed for Pastor Martin Niemoeller at the Lutheran church I attended. Like many Americans, I was hearing for the first time about the courageous clergyman who defied the anti-Christian aims of Adolf Hitler.

At the end of World War II my interest in Niemoeller was intensified by meeting a friend of his, Mrs. Marlene Maertens, a political and religious refugee from Nazi Germany and the widow of a navy classmate of Niemoeller's. I met Martin Niemoeller, church president of Hesse and Nassau, in February of 1956, on a tour with sixteen Americans invited by the West German government to spend a month studying their church and welfare program. I became better acquainted with Pastor Niemoeller and his wife when they came to St. Louis on a visit to America that year. After their next trip to the United States the following year, I received a letter from Mrs. Maertens which began: "Just before he boarded his plane, Martin and I talked of the possibilities of a book about him. We think you are the person to write it."

It is not an easy task to write the story of a man who is still very much alive and whose future actions are unpredictable. Furthermore, the Niemoeller biographer finds much of the extensive material on the man to be untrue. For a writer schooled on a newspaper of high standards where truth and accuracy are taken for granted, it is a shattering experience to encounter distortions and misrepresentations such as are found in any Niemoeller file. In all justice to many honest writers who have written about him, however, it is only fair to explain that Niemoeller has an unparalleled flair for the colorful phrase that lends itself to use out of context as well as a positive genius for "putting his foot in his mouth." On the other hand, there have been praiseworthy efforts in presenting the chapters of the Niemoeller story, notably those of *The Christian Century* magazine.

I have tried in this book to do two things: to clarify some of the misconceptions and misunderstandings that have circulated concerning Martin Niemoeller, and to present a warm, human portrait of a man who is not perfect, not infallible, sometimes contradictory, sometimes maddening, but one who has the courage of a lion and the idealism and sincerity of a dedicated man of God.

I am grateful for the splendid co-operation of the entire Niemoeller family, which took me into the family circle at Number 3 Brentanostrasse in Wiesbaden when I visited them there. I also had the help of many, many Niemoeller partisans and some critics. Experts in the field of religion and the German church struggle aided me immeasurably.

Among those who were especially helpful were the Rev. Drs. Henry Smith Leiper, Samuel McCrea Cavert, Carl Schneider, O. Walter Wagner, Wilhelm Pauck, and Ervine Inglis. In Germany, Drs. Heinz Kloppenburg, Hans Bernd Gisevius, and "the other Pastor Niemoeller," Martin's brother Wilhelm, and my friend, Elisabeth Urbig, of Hilfswerk, helped interpret events. Those whose lives had influenced or been influenced by Pastor Niemoeller—his associate, Franz Hildebrandt; his friends, Mrs. Maertens, Eleanor Kent Browne, and the Rev. Ewart Edmund Turner; fellow concentration prisoners, Colonel Richard Stevens, of England, and former Austrian Chancellor Kurt von Schuschnigg—also contributed their recollections.

CLARISSA START DAVIDSON

Webster Groves, 1959

CONTENTS

GOD'S MAN

The Story of Pastor Niemoeller

1.

NIEMOELLER—TO FRIEND AND FOE

He is one of the most controversial men of our times. To his ardent admirers, his friends and followers, he is a great Christian leader, a man of vision and ideals, to be compared to Albert Schweitzer or Mahatma Gandhi. Over and over again, one hears him described as "the prophet of our century."

His enemies and critics see him quite differently. To them he is a tiresome obstructionist, a habitual minority leader without a positive platform, a tool of the Communists, or, at best, a misguided dreamer, a clergyman out of his field in practical politics.

"People think he is either wonderful or terrible," commented one of his fellow German churchmen. "No one ever says, 'That Martin Niemoeller? Oh, he's all right, I guess.' No one is neutral on the subject of Martin Niemoeller."

He inspires contradictory opinions and his life has been one of contrast. Today, at sixty-seven, he is the Kirchenpraesident, or church president, of the Evangelical Church of Hesse and Nassau, one of the regional divisions of the Protestant Church in Germany. In his youth he was a career man in the German Navy, and during World War I his adventurous activities as an intrepid U-boat commander won him the Iron Cross.

As a clergyman in a fashionable Berlin suburb, he spoke up against the Nazi regime, the "Crooked Cross," and became one

3

of its most publicized victims, for eight years Adolf Hitler's "personal prisoner" in concentration camps.

One might conclude from his present age and position of dignity that Martin Niemoeller has reached the quiet waters, that his stormy days are a thing of the past, but this is not the case. Today he speaks for the Cross of Calvary, and his interpretation of that message is peace on earth and good will toward all men, including those behind the Iron Curtain. His outspoken pacifistic convictions cause him to be at odds with the Bonn West German government, with their Western allies, and with many of the leaders of his own church.

Taking an unpopular stand is nothing new for Martin Niemoeller. A man who knows no fear, either the bodily kind or the more insidious fear of "What will people say?", he spoke out early and emphatically against Hitler in the days when many German churchmen thought it expedient to co-operate with the government. In their opinion, Niemoeller was rash and imprudent. One day after a particularly inflammatory remark, an adviser chided him with a phrase that became famous among his friends.

"Martin, must you say it just that way?" he sighed plaintively.

Others have asked the same question on many occasions since then, but invariably when a matter of principle is involved, Martin Niemoeller feels that he must say it "just that way." In this respect he is a true descendant of Martin Luther, and like Luther, he says in effect, "Here stand I—I can do no other. God help me."

When the war ended, Niemoeller might have settled for his plaudits and privileges as a near-martyr, a church hero who had survived persecution. Instead, he chose the vastly less comfortable role of a leader. Repudiating the Allied system of de-Nazification on the one hand, he alienated many of his countrymen on the other by telling them they were guilty, even the churchgoers, even the self-righteous, even those such as he who had resisted and been jailed. They were guilty of not resisting strongly enough.

"The guilt of the German people exists," he told them, "even if there were no other guilt than that of the six million clay urns, containing the ashes of burnt Jews from all over Europe."

In recent years, Niemoeller has opposed the rearmament and remilitarization of Germany and, instead, has proposed the neutralization and reunification of his country, under UN administration. While his friends and many of his enemies scoff at the idea that he is a Communist sympathizer, he maintains that the Western world can and must live with Russia. In an atomic nuclear age, it is "co-existence or no existence," in his opinion. Like the Rev. Dr. Edwin T. Dahlberg, president of the National Council of Churches, he is a proponent of "massive reconciliation" rather than "massive retaliation." A welcome visitor at pacifist conferences around the world, he has been barred from pulpits in his own country and made unwelcome in England because of his views.

"He is happiest when a storm is raging about his ears" is a phrase often used about Martin Niemoeller, and some have interpreted this to mean that he enjoys a tempest so much that he provokes a controversy if none exists. A German pastor who has known him in war and peace denies this.

"True, some people think of him only as a fighter," said Dr. Heinz Kloppenburg, "but I remember a conversation in the days of the Nazi-church struggle when Pastor Hans Asmussen said, 'We're just a group of *Landsknechte*'—fighters who are professional soldiers and have been fighting so long they don't know what home is. And Martin said, 'I don't feel like a *Landsknecht*. I long to be a *Hausvater* again.' Some see him as a fighter. They do not realize that he fought because it was necessary, but in his heart he longed to be a pastor of his flock, a *Hausvater*."

It is not only his friends who speak in his defense. Bishop

Otto Dibelius of Berlin, one of the leaders in his own church with whom he is frequently at odds over the East-West dispute, wrote in July, 1958, that "Martin Niemoeller's name will be remembered long after those who struggled at his side have been forgotten. . . . It is the name of a man who resolutely staked his whole life for the sake of his faith and for the sake of the true Church."

Quick and caustic of comment, commanding respect for his fidelity, Martin Niemoeller has yet another outstanding characteristic: he can charm the birds from the trees, and many a visitor has approached him in icy reserve only to be melted by the warmth of his smile.

If it were not for the brilliance and frequency of this smile, his slender, finely drawn face might look almost ascetic. Aside from the sensitive features, he is anything but delicate. Ruddy bronze in color, iron gray of hair, he has the trim build and energy of the serviceman who has kept fit. His energy is boundless. He works vigorously, relaxes enthusiastically, and leads a full life in public and private.

Home is at Number 3 Brentanostrasse in Wiesbaden. Its exterior is that of a dignified walled villa, but dazed callers have sometimes found the interior comparable to a scene from *You Can't Take It with You*. A close friend once described a Niemoeller family gathering as "a scene in which only the goldfish are quiet."

There are now five children in the Niemoeller family, although most of them are away much of the time. The eldest daughter, Brigitte, now lives in the United States as does the eldest living son, Hermann, a doctor at Yale University. Hertha, wife of diplomat Wilhelm von Klewitz and mother of three children, lives in the Philippines. Another son, Jan, lives with his wife and son in the nearby town of Buedingen, and the youngest son, Martin, is a student at law school. One son was killed in the war and a daughter died in her teens.

Other members of the family, though unrelated, are Fräulein Dora Schultz, the Niemoellers' housekeeper for many years, her nephew, Hans, and two dachshunds whose pictures the pastor carries in his wallet.

Standing in the midst of the family, as a center of calm and occasionally as referee, is Else Niemoeller—"Mutti" to her husband and children—a serene, white-haired woman who does not seem too perturbed at anything that might happen.

To Number 3 Brentanostrasse come refugees from the Eastern Zone and visitors from all over the world, for the Niemoellers are world travelers who have visited the United States fourteen times since the end of World War II, and other countries on many occasions. One of the criticisms of some of his churchmen is that Martin Niemoeller travels too much and has become too ecumenical-minded, too liberalized by his contacts with the World Council of Churches.

Sometimes visitors are entertained in the living room, at the dinner table, or in the rose garden, but the chosen ones are taken into the family circle in the pastor's study upstairs.

The pastor climbs those stairs two or three at a time. The visitor follows at a more sedate pace and pauses just outside the study with its shelves of books, its family portraits, its framed honorary degrees. For there on the door is a placard, a characteristically humorous touch. It is a picture of a fat elephant illustrating a poem in German, which, translated into English, reads:

> I wish I were an elephant,
> Then would great joy abide.
> I envy not its ivory
> But its thick rugged hide.

There have been times when the hide of an elephant would have helped Martin Niemoeller. There will be more times.

2.

FROM PARSONAGE TO U-BOAT

THE world first heard of Martin Niemoeller in the middle 1930's when he was the pastor of a church in Dahlem, a prosperous suburb on the outskirts of Berlin. Interest was aroused and imaginations captured by the stories of this man of God who had the courage to oppose Adolf Hitler. He was described in the news magazines as a slender, energetic man who walked with a sailor's rolling gait, resembled a businessman more than a minister, and was disconcertingly frank as well as kindly and considerate.

The Rev. Dr. Henry Smith Leiper, American churchman who knew him well, wrote in one of these early sketches, "Religion is a part of his being. In him it is like the heartbeat of a perfectly healthy person. It has not been shaken, it cannot be shaken, not even through suffering and persecution."

All of these qualities, the sailor's gait, the businessman's efficiency, the deep-seated religious convictions were a cumulative effect of Martin Niemoeller's past. His tenacity and stubbornness, admired by some, deplored by others, are not only a part of his past but a part of his heritage.

"The trouble with Niemoeller," said one Lutheran pastor who did not see eye to eye with him, "is that he is a Westphalian. You know what a Westphalian is like? When he comes to a wall, he does not go over it; he goes through it."

Martin Niemoeller is as proud of the state of his birth as

any Texan could be. In region-conscious Germany, where a man can be placed by the inflection of his accent, Martin Niemoeller travels through his adopted land of Hesse and Nassau speaking the dialect of Westphalia like a Texan living in nearby California but clinging to his broad-brimmed hat.

They call it the "Land of the Red Earth," this area of West-phalia between the rivers Rhine and Weser. Its Ruhr is the forge of Germany, but there is more to Westphalia than the Ruhr. There are castles and farm lands, the steep Haarstrang Mountains, and plains of green and golden fields and clusters of trees.

In the midst of one of these plains is the town of Lippstadt spread out in the sunshine. There is none of the surprise of discovery characteristic of many German villages, coyly hidden in the curve of a valley or around a bend in the road. Lippstadt can be seen for miles with its silhouetted housetops and church spires. One spire predominates, that of the Marien-kirche. Its fat steeple seems to rise directly from the end of the straight miles of road approaching the town.

Lippstadt is proud of the fact that it was the first town in Westphalia to accept Martin Luther's Reformation. The Brother House of the town became the first Protestant church. There are newer churches now, the Marienkirche and the Jacobikirche, but the old Bruder Haus remains, a friendly ghost of a building, at the end of the Bruderstrasse.

Next to the Bruder Haus at 13 Bruderstrasse is a gray slate house with stained-glass windowpanes. Affixed to the front is a plaque that reads:

*In diesem Pfarrhause
wurde geboren
Pfarrer DD Martin Niemoeller
am 14 Januar 1892
1892-1900*

It was a few days after January 14, 1892, that Pastor Heinrich Niemoeller and his wife, Pauline, sent out the announcement that "God's goodness has given us a son." The son, appro-
priately enough for a boy born to a Lutheran family in a
Reformation town, was named Martin, and in this house he
spent the first eight impressionable years of his life.

A brick-walled garden extends back from the house, jog-
ging crookedly down toward the Lippe River which crosses
and recrosses Lippstadt with its five twining branches, encir-
cling the town as it once encircled the early fortifications.

The river is olive green in color and the chestnuts and oaks
and willows that border it cast their reflections. Light and
shadow play on its surface. Grass drifts lazily downstream. Its
banks are shady. It is an idyllic scene, and in times of stress
Martin Niemoeller closes his eyes and imagines himself back
there in the happiest period of his life.

There he played, a thin, dark-haired, brown-skinned, active,
energetic, imaginative little boy. One of his first conscious
wishes was for a toy boat. His father ordered it made by the
plumber, out of tin, as a Christmas gift.

Lippstadt, which now has 30,000 inhabitants, at that time
had only 13,000, but from this little town came seven active
professional naval officers in World War I. The reason was
the Lippe River where small boys played at being sailors.

Their play was not all seafaring, however. Around the Lippe
is an area of marshland and meadows which in winter became
a huge skating rink. On the outskirts of town, where the road
runs straight for ten kilometers, the first bicycle races were
held. Here, too, are pastures, where Martin Niemoeller and his
friend, a butcher's son, took the butcher's horse. Martin loved
horses as much as he loved the river.

One especially vivid childhood memory concerns his fondness for a certain horse and how beautiful he thought the curve

of the horse's neck and back. He would stroke it admiringly. In German the word for horse is *"Pferd,"* but in the Westphalian dialect the *p* is not sounded as explosively as in other dialects; it might as well be *"ferd."* When Martin Niemoeller started to school, the first letter he learned to write was *f,* and he connected the sweeping curve of the letter with the curve of the horse's back.

"Now that I can make an *f* I can write *'ferd,'* " he thought happily.

When he learned that the word must be written *"Pferd,"* he felt disappointed, somehow cheated with the whole process of learning.

This was no stolid country boy but a sensitive child. Where did he get this quality? Some say from a French Huguenot ancestor named DeGraes, from whom so many of the Niemoellers get their warm brown eyes. His maternal grandmother was born a DeGraes and married Martin Niemoeller's grandfather, an engineer named Mueller. Grandfather Niemoeller was a teacher who died young; his widow brought up their five boys and two girls, among them Pastor Heinrich Niemoeller, Martin Niemoeller's father.

To Heinrich Niemoeller and Pauline Mueller Niemoeller were born six children: Heinz, who died at four; Martin; Magdalene, now a retired schoolteacher; Pauline, whose husband was a public official until he fell out with Hitler; Wilhelm, "the other Pastor Niemoeller," who joined his brother in the anti-Nazi struggle; and Mary, called Mieze.

The mother was a quiet woman but one whose strong character and high morals made a lasting impression on her children. The father was a big, vital, jovial man. His smiling portraits hang in several rooms in Martin Niemoeller's home. He was a pastor who loved his calling.

"On Sunday I belong in the pulpit," was one of his favorite

sayings, and in sickness and in health he rarely missed a week
of preaching. His sermons were Bible sermons and every year
he collected the neatly handwritten pages and bound them in
a volume. They stretched along the shelves of the library, and
Wilhelm was fond of saying, "Father has two yards of sermons."

There is a German saying:

Pfarrers Kinder
Muellers Vieh
Gedeihen selten
Oder nie.

Loosely translated, it means:

Pastor's children
Miller's beast
Seldom do well
In the least.

The Niemoeller children were not perfect. They got into
scrapes and mischief, and young Martin loved to play Indian,
wearing a feather hat and whooping down Woldemeistrasse,
the business street nearby. Yet their life had its solemn side.
Church bells began and ended each day. There was morning
and evening worship, and God's word was a part of everyday
living.

As the plaque on 13 Bruderstrasse indicates, Martin Niemoeller lived there only eight years. Then his father decided
to improve his pastoral position by moving to Elberfeld, a
larger city. Martin's first reaction to his new home as he looked
out the windows at the tiny back yard with no garden, no river,
was disappointed and frank.

"Oh, Father," he said, "how stupid you were to leave Lipp-stadt and come to Elberfeld."

Even at the age of eight he was not noted for his tact.

For all his first disappointment, Martin Niemoeller learned to love Elberfeld. It was, after all, still in Westphalia and not far from the more scenic homes of his grandparents in Wester-kappeln and Wersen.

Elberfeld is now known as Wuppertal-Barmen. The Nie-moeller home on Arrenbergerstrasse no longer exists, but the church, Trinitatis Kirche, is still there. From home Martin had a long uphill walk through town to the school.

At that time the *Gymnasium,* or secondary school, began after four years of elementary school but because Martin did so well, he was promoted to the *Gymnasium* after three grades. He was an excellent student, good in mathematics, in Latin, so proficient in Greek that he and several fellow students formed a society to read Greek poetry for fun. He was a competent musician, the leader of the band. The only adverse report ever sent home about him was the occasional notation, "Has his mind on other things." He frequently read a more exciting book behind the covers of his dull, easy lessons.

It might have been difficult for him to choose a career except that he had decided long ago on the Lippe River. His brother Wilhelm says that in the room in Elberfeld the walls could not be seen for the naval pictures on them. Martin wanted to join the Merchant Marine but his father said no to that.

"If you must be a sailor, you will go into the Imperial German Navy," he said.

At the age of sixteen Martin took his first steamship voyage, a trip to England for a six-week summer vacation. He loved the ocean travel, and acquired a lifelong love of London with its art galleries and British Museum.

He finished school as the highest-ranking student in his class, thus accorded the honor of making the speech on the graduation program. The point of his speech: while all might not use the Latin and Greek of their formal education, they had learned two things which would serve them well, (1) to think logically, and (2) to work methodically.

Soon he put both of these abilities to work as he entered naval training in April, 1910. After barracks training, the midshipmen were sent on an extended cruise to Tangiers, Morocco, the straits of Gibraltar, Barcelona, Majorca, Bizerte, Tunis, the Adriatic. By New Year's Eve they were in Venice and here young sailor Niemoeller proved himself in another way. After an overly riotous celebration, forty-five of the fifty midshipmen were incapacitated on New Year's Day. The captain and crew officers had been invited to join them for Berliner Pfannkuchen (jelly-filled doughnuts) and grog. (Niemoeller recipe for grog: Rum—a must, sugar—perhaps, water—not necessary.) Preparations had been made for more than fifty guests. Although only five of the fifty were on their feet, the provisions and grog disappeared. One of the rugged five was Niemoeller.

There was work along with the play. They shoveled coal into boilers, sweated as they rowed through the Suez Canal. There were also relaxation and camaraderie. Martin Niemoeller was in seventh heaven.

After a furlough at home to show off their new uniforms— stiff, starched collar, square tie, short jacket with two rows of gold buttons—they returned to Flensburg for another year of work in which seven hours of study a day was augmented by sports, rowing, sailing. At the end of that year they had three weeks of examinations in twelve different categories. Already 20 per cent had been weeded out, but 150 remained. Ratings were established on a point system. One could scrape by with a passing grade but any grade over passing carried a proportionate number of points. When the examinations were over, Martin Niemoeller had 126 points, the top-ranking student in the class.

There had been occasional rumors of war by April of 1912 but they were not taken seriously by the young sailors. The general feeling was that the tense situation would not amount to much. Meanwhile, they attended torpedo school and for a boy of twenty the thrill of commanding a vessel transcended all else.

When the time came to be assigned to a ship, Martin Niemoeller, for selfish reasons, requested a light cruiser rather than a battleship. As highest ranking student he was inevitably in charge of his fellows and responsible for them. He was restive under this burden and wanted to be on a light cruiser with several ensigns, not a big ship with a dozen. When his assignment came, he was not in charge of twelve but twenty-four. The battleship *Thueringen* had its own crew plus that of another battleship not yet finished.

Rumors of war continued to rise and be discounted. When hostilities finally did break out, the crew of the *Thueringen* were on a summer trip in the Norwegian fjords and their first reaction was one of disappointment that their holiday was over.

The first year of war was one of complete boredom. Noth-thing happened. Everyone tried to get another appointment.

In November, 1915, Martin Niemoeller secured his wish and was transferred to submarine duty, first as watchkeeper on the *Vulkan,* then to the *U73,* a mine layer. This, too, was disappointing at first for the *U73* was laid up for repairs and even in top-notch condition was not much of a boat. Its men disrespectfully referred to it as a "floating coffin." But seaworthy or not, it took off on its first mission on March 30, 1916, to the Mediterranean.

Besieged by rough weather, they wore oilskins constantly,

were lashed to the rails; the galley gave up cooking. Finally they reached the Mediterranean and with calm daring laid their mines under the very nose of the enemy. When they surfaced one day in the midst of French fishing boats, they ran up the French tricolor and exchanged nonchalant waves of greeting. Meanwhile, a Norwegian steamer with 5,000 tons of wheat had struck one of their mines.

Plagued with engine trouble, they skulked through the straits of Gibraltar, crash-dived frequently to avoid unfriendly warships, and succeeded in laying twenty-two mines in Valetta Harbor on a calm night with the town and dockyards a blaze of light. Three British warships and an armed yacht went down there.

On May 2 they were decorated and returned to Kiel and only realized the extent of their endeavor when the lieutenant commander looked at them with astonishment as they reported in.

"You still alive?" he asked. "We thought the *U73* was lost long ago."

By now the cold war was pretty well over for U-boat officer Martin Niemoeller.

3.

FROM U-BOAT TO PULPIT

In the fall of 1917 Martin Niemoeller's U-boat was lying off the coast of Dakar when a French steamer sailed into view. They exchanged gunfire but the French ship outdistanced the submarine and got away. A few years ago Albert Schweitzer wrote to Niemoeller and asked if, by any chance, he had been on a German submarine that almost sank a French ship on that occasion. Schweitzer was personally interested: he had been on the French ship. Niemoeller wrote that it had to be his U-boat, since it was the only one around at that time. Schweitzer replied:

"So—you were really after my life! Thank God you didn't get me or you would have robbed yourself of one of your stanchest comrades in your fight for peace."

The fact that Martin Niemoeller and Albert Schweitzer were battling on opposite sides illustrates to both of them the futility of war.

Some of Niemoeller's critics have accused him of being a happy warrior and pointed to the fact that his navy logs show a spirit of excitement and enthusiasm. In view of his later life, they feel he made a mistake in becoming involved in a shooting war. To his admirers this is the height of idiocy. He was a navy career man, war broke out, he fought in defense of his country, a procedure which some Americans consider commendable only when the country happens to be America. For

Martin Niemoeller it was natural to fight for his homeland and certainly normal to prefer victory to defeat. He found war a dirty business but, as he has pointed out, "in wartime one does not become a pacifist."

As deadly in war as he has been tireless in his peace efforts, he was known as "The Scourge of Malta," and ran up records for Allied shipping losses. He sees no conflict between this discharge of duty and his present sentiments on the uselessness of war.

Some people would like to establish a point of conversion in his life during World War I. They conclude that he must have gone into service a ruthless killer and come out a man of Christ. Actually Martin Niemoeller was a dedicated Christian when he entered the Navy and has never changed.

However, there were incidents in the war that pointed to its senselessness. In January, 1917, Niemoeller was on a new submarine, the *U39,* in the eastern Mediterranean when they struck a French troopship. Within minutes the sea was dotted with men swimming for their lives. A destroyer and a trawler appeared on the scene to rescue the survivors. The submarine had one torpedo left.

"Stand by," the captain shouted. "First tube ready."

"No, Captain," Niemoeller protested. "We can't torpedo that destroyer again. It's not right."

The captain looked at him as if he thought he was mad.

"But every soldier they pick up will be fighting our men in a few days," he said.

Niemoeller persisted and won out. The rescue mission was allowed to go on. And that night a lengthy discussion ensued in the wardroom. What was "right" in war?

"We realized," he later wrote in his autobiography, "from this single experience of ours something of the tragedy which it involved, which no single man could, of his own volition, avert. . . . A moratorium on Christianity! How often theological circles talked of it. We junior officers knew nothing and cared less about theological problems. But we did see that situations involving spiritual bankruptcy did arise in which it was utterly impossible to preserve a clear conscience."

However, war went on. And when Niemoeller returned from this trip he wore the Iron Cross.

Martin Niemoeller was sent to take special training in Ber lin, a shore experience he did not appreciate, though it had its compensations. In Berlin he began seeing a girl from Elberfeld, Else Bremer, sister of his best friend, Hermann Bremer. They had known each other for years. Else's first conscious memory of Martin Niemoeller was his presence at her brother's twelfth birthday party. She recalled him as a "boy who was dark and very quick about everything and ate an enormous amount of cake."

One of five children of a doctor, Else had been a schoolteacher and now was studying at the University of Berlin. Drawn together by home ties, by the war, by mutual loneliness, and in those days of belt-tightening, by occasional hunger, they saw a lot of each other that warm sunny spring of 1917. Often they brought each other a token gift of food, a piece of bread, a sack of cherries. Very soon they were in love.

But Martin Niemoeller, like many servicemen, did not believe in marriage in wartime. It would not do, he told Else brusquely. They must not see each other again. She thought that was the end of the matter.

He went away on another mission and she did not hear from him, but she heard a great deal about him.

His new submarine, the *U151*, had several spectacular successes, among them the capture of a shipload of badly-needed copper. Niemoeller was a hero at home, given a royal welcome on his return, and a special leave, but he did not go to Berlin. Instead, he left to take command of his own submarine, the *UC67*. Again his exploits were successful although Germany's war effort was fast becoming a lost cause. In July he had another leave and this time he arrived in Berlin on Else's birthday, July 20. He brought her a huge bouquet of roses.

"Now we are engaged," he told her in no uncertain terms.

"You haven't asked me," she protested.

"You will not be asked," he said.

But there were complications. A young naval officer had to have a certain amount of money in order to marry. Martin's kindly father went to his fiancée's father to see if they could help the young people. Between the two families they raised the money. As the conference went on, Else waited on the front porch of her home, in fear and trepidation. Then her father-in-law opened the door, smiling.

"Now give me the first kiss," he said.

Their joy was marred by news that her brother Hermann had been lost in the Irish Sea. Her mother suffered a collapse, and Else herself, frail from lack of food, became ill.

Before he went back to duty, Martin Niemoeller talked to his other good friend, Hans Emsmann. Just before the train left to take Niemoeller back to his port of embarkation, Emsmann leaned through the window for a few last words.

"If the war is lost," he said, "it will certainly not be due to anything you and I have done."

Martin never saw him again. Emsmann was lost in the last submarine of the war to go down.

The war was lost and those who continued to fight knew it. Talk revolved chiefly about what the future might hold. One night Niemoeller and a boyhood acquaintance, Karli Topp, were on the bridge when the question of future vocations came up.

"I might become a minister," Niemoeller said casually.

The thought surprised him even as he voiced it. Since the age of five he had thought of nothing but a navy career.

A month later the war was over and the men returned to

find that a revolution had taken place, the monarchy had been overthrown, and a republic set up. Confusion and conflict bordered on chaos. Momentarily Martin Niemoeller regretted that he had come home. Perhaps another country would be the answer. Many other Germans had the same idea, and Argentina began to be spoken of as the promised land for those who felt their homeland held no promise.

Standing at a window, weeping for her lost son as the New Year of 1919 was rung in, Else's mother asked Martin Niemoeller the question that was in every mind.

"Do you really think, Martin, that things will come out all right in Germany?"

"Of course they will," he answered with assurance.

But he was to write later in his autobiography that all he could see at the time was "not a road but a winding path leading through a dense mass of bushes."

He returned to the Navy where he received orders to take two submarines to England in compliance with the terms of the Armistice. His reply became part of German history.

"I have sailed in submarines for three years, fighting against England, sir," he told his commodore. "I have neither sought nor concluded this armistice. As far as I am concerned, the people who promised our submarines to England can take them over. I will not do it."

There was a moment of silence.

"Very well," the commodore said finally. "I will give the order to another officer."

It was a moral victory but it did not make his future course any easier. Resignation from the Navy was a foregone conclusion. He and Else talked earnestly about a possible move and wrote to the Argentine Association in Berlin and the Ibero-America Institute in Hamburg. They began to study Spanish.

Just when it seemed there was no solution, a letter came

from Martin's uncle, Ludwig Mueller, in Westerkappeln. He understood the young people were considering emigrating to the Argentine to try farming. Why go there when there were farms at home? A man on a neighboring farm, Wieligmann by name, would take Martin on as an apprentice.

The idea had great appeal. There was a general back-to-the-farm movement in Germany at this time. The land seemed to offer basic security. Perhaps in this simple way, Martin Niemoeller told himself, he could help in the rebirth of his country. He wrote back that he would accept the offer.

On March 27, 1919, he submitted his formal resignation to the Navy. It was a painful moment, but at least the path through the woods began to seem clearer.

On April 20, 1919, a simple home wedding was held for Else Bremer and Martin Niemoeller, with Pastor Heinrich Niemoeller performing the ceremony. On May 5 Martin Niemoeller reported to the Wieligmann farm to work, late in the afternoon. He sowed oats, greased four wagons, was in bed by ten. The next morning he was up at dawn, carting and spreading manure for a beet field. As he followed the plow for the first time, he thought inevitably of the Bible verse, "No man having put his hand to the plow and then looking back is worthy of the Kingdom of God." He did not look back.

It was a ninety-acre farm, part wood, part meadow, one third in cultivation. There were no tractors in those days but many horses. A favorite task of Martin's was the early-morning mowing and gathering of green fodder for the cattle as the rising sun lighted the sky.

He worked every day from sunup to after sundown except on Sunday, which he spent with Else and the relatives in Westerkappeln. As summer came on, the work was heavier with potatoes and turnips to hoe. Then came haymaking, and men in wide-brimmed hats, women with kerchiefs tied on their heads joined the forces of extra haymakers, starting early in the morning, when the fields were still wet with dew.

Although the work was hard, Martin Niemoeller found it satisfying. He was losing the feeling of bitterness he had experienced at the end of the war, beginning to find new ties binding him to his homeland. It was almost as if the field of his life was being plowed to prepare it for something new.

Else went to work as an apprentice to a farm wife, no easy work for a girl brought up to teach school. The young couple saw little of each other, for although the farms were only five miles apart, the connecting roads were winding and time was scarce. They looked forward to the day when they might have their own farm.

Then suddenly in the fall of 1919 a new specter loomed, the beginning of inflation. Prices rose steeply. Farms were out of their reach; even a few acres of land were beyond their capital. The most they could hope to do was rent a small place. Impatiently Martin Niemoeller began turning over substitute ideas in his mind.

He considered other professions. Teaching? Perhaps. But schools were under government control and he did not find the new government to his liking. No, teaching was not the answer. One night, walking to Westerkappeln to visit his uncle, he stopped to talk to the local clergyman, the Rev. Johann zu Settel. Later, as he continued on his way, he stopped suddenly. A recollection flashed through his mind: the night on the bridge of the *UC67* when he had said to Karli Topp, "I might become a minister."

Instantly it was crystal clear. Of course, this was the answer. Now he saw why he had been dissatisfied. He had withdrawn, escaped from responsibility instead of accepting it. Work on the farm had healed old wounds and refreshed him, but it was not the job he had to do. He hurried to tell Else his decision.

A few nights later, sitting with farmer Wieligmann in the

pigsty waiting for a sow to farrow, he confessed that he wanted a release from service. He promised to stay until the potato crop was in. Then, in a drenching rainstorm, he walked over to see the Rev. Johann zu Settel to ask if he would teach him Hebrew.

Martin Niemoeller undertook his studies for the ministry precisely as he had done everything in his life—with thoroughness, wholehearted preoccupation, and the intention of being a success. It was not easy for a married man some years out of school to satisfy the necessary language and other requirements in a short space of time.

He and Else moved into two upper rooms in the home of the Mueller relatives for several months as he studied Hebrew day and night, and then in December, 1919, to three attic rooms in Muenster where he began his theological studies. By this time their first baby was on the way, due to arrive in April.

In March all normal life was interrupted by the abortive Kapp *Putsch* against the Weimar Republic. The Spartacists or Communists in the Rhineland-Westphalia industrial area seized power and many nationalists, like former Navy man Niemoeller and his fellow students, went out to fight on the side of the revolutionaries. For a few brief weeks he was a military man again and his wife was less than enthusiastic because he was at "the front," instead of at her side, when their baby girl, Brigitte, was born. Then suddenly the *Putsch* was over and the government restored.

Studies went on, sometimes in the company of brother Wilhelm, who was also preparing for the ministry and often visited them. The year 1921 brought more uprisings and unrest and for the Niemoellers personal tragedy. Their second child was born dead, and although kind female relatives assured Else Niemoeller that "these things happen," she brooded over it.

Near the end of 1921 a big event occurred in the life of

the student pastor. On December 15 he preached his first sermon.

He knew it was not a complete success and smarted over the knowledge. All week long he thought about it. Toward the end of the week he telephoned his father in Elberfeld and asked if he could preach in his pulpit. That Sunday he mounted to the pulpit for the second time and now as he read the text—"My soul doth magnify the Lord"—he did so with a humbler spirit, trying to convey the glad tidings of the Advent season. He felt he had learned the truth of the maxim, "The preacher must first preach to himself."

Inflation grew steadily in the spring of 1922 and the young couple were driven to extremes to try to meet its demands. They tried to find a purchaser for the only object of real value they owned, a 1545 Luther Bible. Luckily they were not able to sell it and it remains in their possession today.

Again their family increased, this time a boy named for Niemoeller's friend, Emsmann—Hans Jochen. To make ends meet, Martin Niemoeller went to work as a laborer on the railroad. His fellow workers were a rough lot and not too receptive to a college boy, but after one fight, which he won, he found himself accepted. Months later, traveling by train, Else Niemoeller was puzzled when the train slowed down and a group of men alongside the track began waving enthusiastically at her husband.

"My gang," Pastor Niemoeller said proudly, waving back.

Early in 1923 he completed his thesis and in April passed his examinations, thus attaining his assistant's position with the local minister, a Rev. Mr. Kaehler. Inflation was going up faster than his income. Else spent her evenings picking gold lace off his old uniforms so they could sell it to the jeweler. Desperately Martin Niemoeller tried additional job after job, on the railway, in a bank, back at the railway.

By October, 1923, money was burning in people's hands

and lost half its value in half a day. Paper mills and printing presses could not keep pace with the need for supplies. A wild scramble ensued for real goods of all kinds. Workers took suitcases to work with them to bring home their wages in the form of bread.

In the midst of this chaotic situation came a real offer of help, a job with the Westphalian Innere Mission. It was not exactly what Martin Niemoeller had wanted from the ministry. He had hoped for the peaceful, orderly work of a parish and this was an administrative job. But it was a living, a living which his growing family badly needed.

The following June, 1924, he was formally ordained, and on the same day he christened his third child, six-month-old Heinz Hermann Niemoeller. The desk in the attic apartment served as an altar. On it was a crucifix, candlesticks, and a font. Behind it was the ensign of the submarine *UC67*. In all, the scene typified the more than five years of postwar struggle of the young pastor and his family. The text he chose was equally symbolic of his emotions:

"Oh, give thanks unto the Lord for He is good; for His mercy endureth forever."

4.

THE PASTOR OF DAHLEM

SEVEN hundred years of the love of God surrounds you as you sit on one of the simple wooden, stone-supported benches in the yard of the Annenkirche, historic St. Anne's church in Berlin-Dahlem. Seven hundred years, and the carefully tended graves of the faithful from former congregations. Throughout the churchyard are the neat mounds, in typical German fashion, as colorful as a botanical garden with their blue ageratum and pink begonias. Old trees shade the yard. A breeze blows. In the background can be heard the rhythmic clip-clip-clip of the gardener's shears.

Else Niemoeller fell in love with this church and especially with the churchyard the first time she came to Dahlem. Among the rows of headstones marking the names of old Annenkirche families, Kirchner, Marks, Zarnack, Schilling, Aderhold, Bartsch, Rummel, Schulz, is a bare spot big enough for two graves. These were set aside for Martin and Else Niemoeller.

This was long ago, and the Niemoellers may never return to Dahlem to be buried. But whether they do or not is unimportant. Dahlem belongs to Martin Niemoeller and Martin Niemoeller belongs to Dahlem because it was there that he made history.

It was in 1931 that he left his job as mission administrator to become a pastor at the Annenkirche. His reason for changing his position was not the customary one of advancement

27

up the ladder of success but a casual occurrence on which his entire future hung.

He had done a good job in the Innere Mission, the business office of the church, with its several hundred institutions and administrative divisions. Good at organizational work, trained in navy efficiency, he had established a splendid record by reorganizing the Home Mission bank, setting up new institutions for the sick and aged, founding a hospital in his home town of Lippstadt for the study of tuberculosis of the bone— coincidentally his mother subsequently became a patient—and managing all the many details of his office.

Part of his job involved close contact with one of Germany's church leaders, Friedrich von Bodelschwingh, director of Bethel. Bethel is a remarkable place, a small self-contained city dedicated to the care of the handicapped. It was founded in 1867 for the care of a handful of epileptics, one of the first places to treat them as sick instead of feeble-minded victims. It grew into a town in which every trade is practiced, a community where the sick live and work and worship. "Work, not alms," is their slogan.

The Pastor von Bodelschwingh who founded Bethel died in 1910 and it was his son, the second Von Bodelschwingh, who became Martin Niemoeller's friend, then and in the Nazi days to follow, when Adolf Hitler asked that the handicapped be put to death and Von Bodelschwingh resisted the order. "When Hitler asked what the church had done for the uplifting of people," the Dean of Chichester wrote, "men pointed to Bethel."

This friendship meant a great deal to Martin Niemoeller. It was one of the happy aspects of his job.

There were other happy aspects. The family prospered. They built a new house in Muenster and, characteristically, Martin Niemoeller consulted and worked with the architects on every detail. It was a house far in advance of its time, a split-level arrangement with his office on a lower floor, living quarters planned around a central hall so that one did not have to pass through any room to get to the others, a large terrace for the children's play activities.

Their family grew here. To join Brigitte, Jochen, and Hermann, Jan, a third son, was born on December 11, 1925, Hertha, on July 8, 1927, Jutta, on November 15, 1928. Niemoeller, the church administrator, had still not quite gotten over his days in the Navy. His two younger daughters were named for vessels on which he had sailed.

They had two housemaids, usually girls sent by the church-welfare organizations in need of training, but nevertheless a help with the growing family. They were able to buy a car, a Hanomag, and take vacation trips south to the Bavarian Alps, north to the Frisian Islands. Martin Niemoeller was a member of the City Council, the only Protestant to be so honored in Catholic Muenster. All things considered, for a couple who had known discouragement and material hardship, they had won tangible social and financial success.

And yet Martin Niemoeller was not satisfied.

"What good did it do me to study to become a pastor when all I do is practice law and banking?" he sometimes grumbled.

Else, while she tried to encourage him, was not entirely satisfied with their life. His job required him to travel a great deal. Sometimes he was away as many as two hundred days a year.

Then along came one of those minor frustrations, a little thing which turned out to be the last straw. He had asked for an assistant, a certain social worker he felt he needed to lighten the administrative load of his work. The board demurred, hesitated, put him off. He flared up and in sudden anger told them that perhaps it would be better if he were to make a change. They still did not take action. He submitted his resignation as of July 1, 1931. It was then early spring.

His father was furious.

"You have six children," he reminded his son, "and where are you going to go? You should not have given notice to your board until you had found a new position." Then, cooling off a little, he suggested that his son write letters of application to some of the churches in Westphalia. Young Pastor Niemoeller was too proud to do this.

"The churches in Westphalia know me," he said. "If they want me, they will ask for me."

Several churches did ask for him but for one reason or another the situations did not suit him. Then, just as time was growing perilously short, he received an unexpected letter from the church in Prussia. A third pastorate was being created in the Berlin-Dahlem area. He was asked to consider the post.

He was taken aback. He had never thought of going so far from Westphalia. Berlin was an adventurous idea, a challenge for a provincial pastor to try a big city. He wrote back:

"I do not say no. I would like to talk to you."

He drove the Hanomag car to Dahlem where he had a satisfactory interview. He accepted on condition that he could find a place for his family to live. Before he left, a seven-room apartment had been located on Podbielskiallee. It was not like a private home, it had no garden, but the children were excited at the idea of moving to Berlin.

And so the Niemoellers moved to Berlin-Dahlem, the pastor, his wife, six children, and an aquarium of fish which he himself carried.

They were greeted on their first night in Dahlem by Schwester Gertrud, one of the sisters at the Gemeinde Haus, or church building, across from the church. She had this hopeful word of greeting:

"Every pastor who goes to this pulpit grows on this pulpit."

Martin Niemoeller was no exception. He loved his new job, the life of a pastor, a *Hausvater,* freed from the irksome details of a businessman. He set himself to the ambitious task of visiting every family in the congregation. It took several years but it brought him multiple returns later on. When difficulties arose, the new pastor had many friends.

The family did not stay long in the apartment at 20 Podbielskiallee. It was too confining. The children played a bowling game in the long corridors, and the neighbors complained.

One of the elderly pastors who had been ailing died, and they moved into the parsonage next to the church on Cecilienallee, which is now known as Pacelliallee, half a block from Dahlem's main street, the Koenigin Luisestrasse. It was a solid, cream-colored structure, built in 1912, with twelve rooms, a comfortable bay-windowed recess in the pastor's study just right for a desk, a small garden in front and a larger one bordering on a schoolyard in back. They moved in, and life settled down to a peaceful pattern.

On Tuesdays and Fridays Else Niemoeller walked along the Koenigin Luisestrasse to Dahlem Dorf, the village, to go to the bakery, the shops, the outdoor markets. The house and children occupied the rest of her time, and often on Sunday mornings, after she had finished getting them ready, she would run down the walk between the flowery graves, reaching the church quite breathless just as the service began.

At Christmas time, 1931, a new church was dedicated, the Jesus Christus Kirche, or Church of Jesus Christ, one train stop beyond Dahlem, in a more park-like residential area. It is a handsome building of simple modern design, its only adornment a heroic figure of the Christ, arms outstretched in welcome.

Much as Else Niemoeller loved the Annenkirche with its Gothic vaulted ceiling, its medieval, raised center platform and niches with gold statues, she loved the Jesus Christus Kirche, too, and had a strange, special feeling about the new church.

She felt as if the church had been built especially for her husband, and in some respects she was right. It was to serve as a stage on which the part of the drama of the struggle between church and state, nazidom and Christendom, was to take place, a drama in which Martin Niemoeller was to be one of the principal actors.

5.

THE HOPE OF HITLER

"ONE must realize that there were two Martin Niemoellers," Dr. Hans Bernd Gisevius, of Berlin, once said of his good friend. "There was the church Niemoeller but there was also the Niemoeller who was one of the main people of the resistance long before that word was used. What did we call ourselves then? I suppose we might have been called the Opposition or anti-Nazi or anti-Gestapo. But there was no such big name as resistance."

In the story of the resistance to Adolf Hitler Dr. Hans Bernd Gisevius is a colorful figure. He was a member of the Gestapo, sent to report on Niemoeller, when he first approached the pastor at a Sunday service and said softly, "I am supposed to be watching you, but don't worry, I'm on your side." He did not stay in the Gestapo but managed, in one way or another, to remain in the Nazi government and yet keep in constant communication with the forces that time and again plotted to overthrow the Nazis.

In his book, *To the Bitter End,* he tells of the adventures and intrigue of this period, of his eventual discovery and near disaster. Forced to go into hiding, no easy trick for a man who is a physical giant in appearance, he found refuge in the heart of Berlin, then managed to escape in a boxcar on the last train to Switzerland. After the war he returned to marry the woman who had helped to hide him.

Gisevius, an early member of the resistance, has identified Niemoeller as also among the first members of the resistance. This is important because from time to time there have appeared irresponsible statements referring to Niemoeller as a "Nazi party member," a German who "went along" with Hitler and "never really objected to the Nazi ideology," but only to its ambitions concerning the church. These imply that his resistance was a late-blooming thing.

This much should be established first of all:

Martin Niemoeller was never a member of the Nazi party.

This is not to say that he did not believe in many of the things in which the Nazi party believed. The Nazi party found favor with many Protestants from 1921 on, when it placed Article 24 in its party program. It read:

"We demand freedom for all religious confessions within the state, in so far as they are not a danger to it and do not offend the moral feelings of the German race. The party as such stands for positive Christianity."

It was an attractive phrase, "positive Christianity," and many Protestants were attracted by it. Among them was Pastor Wilhelm Niemoeller of Bielefeld, Martin Niemoeller's brother. He joined the Nazi party in 1924 and suggested that his brother join along with him.

"I considered it," Martin Niemoeller has freely admitted. "I had come back from the war in 1918 and found everything changed. Like many a member of the younger generation, I wanted to have more of a voice in government. And like many of the younger generation, I was rapidly becoming more and more disappointed with the Weimar Republic. But I was not sure of the advisability of a pastor joining any political party. I came to the conclusion that it was best not to be affiliated. I did vote for Hitler in 1924 and again in 1928."

What was this appeal which the Nazi party had for the brothers Niemoeller and other Protestants in the 1920's? Here one must understand something of German church and state history.

The Weimar Republic found disfavor with Protestant church groups because of its adherence to the liberal principle of the separation of church and state. In the United States this principle, proclaimed in the Constitution, is accepted so generally that it seems a kind of heresy to question it. Germany has precisely the opposite tradition.

The bond between church and state goes back to the earliest days of the church in Germany. "Altar and Throne" was the familiar slogan. Both Catholic and Protestant churches are in large part today, and were in the time of the Hohenzollerns, supported by public tax monies collected by the government. Until 1918 the Kaiser was the head of the Protestant Church, the *summus episcopus*, just as the Queen of England is the head of the Church of England. Church families regularly prayed for the *Landesherr* and his house. The "public schools" were, and still are, the schools supported by taxes but operated by the churches.

One must say "churches" rather than church, even in speaking of the Protestant Church in Germany for it was not a united church. Even Martin Luther had not been able to accomplish that. The early Protestant churches were supported by princelings. Up until 1933 the twenty-eight provincial churches—*Landeskirchen*—corresponded to the federal states that made up the united Germany. In 1922 there had been an attempt at unification through the establishment of the German Evangelical Federation, but the *Landeskirchen* continued to be the real administrative units.

Confessionally, Protestants belonged to one of three groups: the Lutheran, the Reformed or Calvinistic, and the United which sought to bring the two conflicting groups together. But church membership depended less on acceptance of a confession, as we know it in the United States, than upon birth into a particular type of church. Churchmanship came automatically with citizenship.

When the republic supplanted the monarchy at the end of World War I, the union between church and state came to an end. State support, to which the church had been accustomed since the sixteenth century, ceased. This did not mean that all financial aid was withdrawn from the church by the state. In many instances there was historic precedent which was honored. For example, in Prussia, the Hohenzollerns had confiscated church property in order to finance the Napoleonic Wars and in return made annual contributions to the church. The republic continued these payments.

Many of the state churches continued the practice of church taxation, adding a percentage onto the state income tax, and made arrangements with the finance departments of their state to collect the taxes. But the tax collector had no way to compel the payment of these taxes or punish the failure to pay. The Protestants found themselves suffering financially under this new precept of separation of church and state.

For the Roman Catholics, the change was less drastic. The head of their church had always been the pope in Rome, not the emperor in Germany. Their organization was international in scope, not national. Moreover, as a political group, the Zentrum or Center party, they provided a formidable bloc. Konrad Adenauer, then mayor of Cologne, was a Zentrum leader, and a part of the animosity between Adenauer and Kirchenpraesident Niemoeller today can be traced back to those days. Catholics filled many political posts. Protestants felt they were exerting disproportionate political influence.

Many felt the same way about the Jews, and apologists for the Nazis produced statistics to prove how many Jews had been appointed to high places of political influence. The Weimar Republic encouraged the immigration of Jews from Russia and Poland, and Germany, a country that once had had less overt anti-Semitism than any other country in Europe began to show the first signs of that cancer.

This situation was not helped by a long and sensational series of trials of men accused of graft in postwar goods in the early days of the republic. The defendants were Jews, the chief prosecutor, Karl Helfferich, one of the leaders of the conservative National German party with which men such as the Niemoellers sympathized. Many Protestants began to associate judaism with marxism and marxism with godlessness. They connected judaism with the activities of the communist groups, which encouraged people to try companionate marriage, to avoid their church taxes, to leave the church.

Many of the Protestant churchmen began looking wistfully back to the days of church and state. Bereft of leadership, they were ripe for someone to lead them.

"In the early thirties," writes Michael Power in *Religion in the Reich,* "there was already this great unharnessed, semi-religious restlessness, believing deeply but vaguely in the greatness of German blood and the glory of German soil. . . . When the Fuehrer demanded that they should subordinate everything to loyalty, he only demanded what millions were eager, even anxious, to give."

One of the first public proclamations of the Nazi party was that the abolition of the monarchy had been a mistake. So thought many Protestants, among them Martin Niemoeller. The Nazi party called for the restoration of the empire. With this, too, Niemoeller agreed. The party said that the Evangelical Church should once again become a strong factor in the life of the nation. Certainly Pastor Niemoeller agreed with this.

All in all it seemed as if this National Socialist party had much to offer, thus reasoned the Protestants. To be sure it had its anti-Semitic group but there are people of prejudice everywhere. The Nazis also had such men as Alfred Rosenberg, editor of the *Voelkischer Beobachter,* who had written the

book *Myths of the Twentieth Century,* proclaiming a faith
based on Nordic blood, but—the Protestants may have reasoned—such men as Rosenberg were part of the lunatic fringe,
not to be taken seriously.

Basically, Martin Niemoeller believed, the Nazis were interested, as he was, in God and Germany. Later on it turned out
they were only half in agreement.

Along with their problems from without the Protestant
churches in Germany were experiencing problems from within.
There were many who felt that the church had become too remote, too involved with dogma and abstractions. The Swiss
theologian, Karl Barth, found wide favor when he challenged
this subjectivism and proclaimed that the essence of Christianity is, and always must be, the Cross.

In addition to theological dissatisfaction there was dissatisfaction with the bureaucracy of church government. The leaders were out of touch with the people. There was no genuine
interest in church affairs. The organization of twenty-eight
churches was cumbersome. Some, Martin Niemoeller among
them, would have preferred to see one united church. And yet
Martin Niemoeller did not go along with the group that was to
become the proponent of one church, one state, one people,
the German Christians.

The German Christian group had its beginning in 1932,
under Joachim Hossenfelder, a vigorous and persuasive speaker
who put marxism and godlessness on one side, National Socialism and the German Christians on the other.

"Christian faith," he said, "is a heroic, manly thing. God
speaks in blood and *Volk* a more powerful language than he
does in the idea of humanity."

The stronghold of the German Christians was Thuringia,
Luther's own country, and sometimes they were called Thurin-
gian Christians. When they organized, they asked Hitler's permission to call themselves Evangelical National Socialists.

Hitler rejected the idea and suggested as an alternative German Christians.

Shortly after the Niemoellers came to Dahlem church elections were held, and for the first time on the Dahlem church board, out of the group of ten there were two representing the new group. Niemoeller did not like them but he was not too concerned about them. He did not think they would get very far in Dahlem, a settled and conservative community.

But although all the Protestants did not see eye to eye with the Protestant group within the Nazi party, the desire for something new was great. In American parlance, Protestants generally felt it was "time for a change."

When Martin Niemoeller preached on New Year's Day, 1933, he began his sermon with these words:

"May God be with us in the new year, dear brethren, and may the Lord Jesus Christ comfort us! For we shall have great need of His comfort in the year across whose threshold we have just stepped, this year which lies before us like an unknown country."

Before the year was one month old, on January 30, 1933, Adolf Hitler had assumed the chancellorship, and, like many other Protestants, Martin Niemoeller greeted the Nazi victory with a heart full of thanksgiving and hope, a feeling of optimism that a change had been made and the change would be for the good.

6.

RELIGIOUS "FIFTH COLUMN"

WHEN Hitler came to power, many a Protestant churchman thought, 'Now we can hold our heads high again,' " said Professor Franz Hildebrandt, who was one of them. "We were very shortly disillusioned. Hitler worked on the church just as he worked on Czechoslovakia and Norway, by means of a fifth column."

The religious fifth column, the German Christians, went into action promptly. Bernhard Rust, the new Prussian minister of education, promptly appointed Hossenfelder as adviser. Four days later Hossenfelder preached on the wondrous works of God in Germany, how after fourteen years of desolation God had chosen his man, a man of "purity, piety, energy, and strength of character, our Adolf Hitler."

It was a strange and contradictory year, that year of 1933 in Germany. One American churchman, Dr. Charles Macfarland, who visited there, reported that the stock answer given to misgivings he expressed was, "You must remember that this is a revolution."

There were churchmen, German as well as American, who had misgivings. But once you have voted for a change in administration, you don't start attacking the man you've just put in office within two months after he has come to power. It's normal to reason, "Let's give him a chance." Especially was this true of the Protestant clergy with its history of cooperation with the state.

"Also," Dr. Gisevius has pointed out, "some people felt that Von Hindenburg was still there and he knew his responsibility to law and Christendom. Some of the stories must be exaggerated.

"Others felt, 'Well, it's too bad the turn things are taking but it's not my job to criticize. And nothing will happen in my own nice, well-regulated community.' "

Nothing was threatening Martin Niemoeller's nice, well-regulated Dahlem, but he did not hesitate to criticize only two months after Hitler came to power. There were many who felt his criticism was premature.

"When our German church became a nation," he said in a sermon on March 5, the first Sunday in Lent, 1933, "God gave it as soul the Christian faith. Our national development, whether we like it or not, has been inwardly based upon Christianity and from this Christianity of the German national soul has come all the forces which made our nation develop and grow.

"This nation—our nation—will either be a Christian nation or it will cease to exist.

"For that reason we can and must ask the nation's political leaders to take this vital interest into account and not to be deluded into thinking that the question of religion can ever be a private matter among us. If such a mistaken policy is ever adopted—and we have surely been heading in that direction—our nation will dissolve into atoms; it will be denationalized and its historical existence will be at an end. And in thus ceasing to be, our nation would not be dying a natural death but would be guilty of committing suicide. . . .

"Just as a healthy man is not sure of his life merely because he is healthy, and just as he may lose his life through an accident or through the treachery of others, so our nation is not sure of its life and so our nation can lose its life through superior force or through the violence of others. But just as an intelligent man knows these contingencies and yet at the same time takes care of his health, so must we as a nation know them and yet realize and bear our responsibility for the health of our nation."

This was Niemoeller's flat statement to the alarming trend of anti-Christianity among the new powers. On March 23 Adolf Hitler made his program speech to the Reichstag. It was enough to quiet any fears.

Said Hitler, "The National Government sees in the two Christian confessions most vital factors in the survival of our nationality . . . their rights will not be touched. . . . The National Government will accord and secure to the Christian Confessions the influence that is due to them in schools and education. Its aim is the genuine interrelation of church and state."

Many took this as an indication that Hitler was truly a "man of God." In addition, Hitler had an emotional impact. The Nazis marched through the streets with flags, music, and songs. Their meetings made much of the psychology of mass enthusiasm. The sudden silences when the Fuehrer stood before them only heightened the drama.

Something like a religious revival started. Storm troopers en masse began attending church. It was not unusual to have mass weddings of couples who had never bothered getting formally married. Was it sincere conversion? Few cared to distinguish.

Some churchmen did criticize this revival. Church papers in the spring of 1933 carried articles on the impropriety of using churches for demonstrations by storm troopers.

But there were other pastors who, being only human,

thought, "I've been preaching to empty churches and disinterested congregations. If this man can bring the masses back to church, he is truly the answer to my prayer."

According to the dean of Chichester, Martin Niemoeller was not deceived. Wrote the dean:

> The easy slogans aroused in him, not hope but fear. Rebirth of Christianity would not be brought about by large-scale propaganda schemes. It was easy to make much of Christian charity and church-welfare work. These were but human works, a sort of Christian sugaricing without the one thing needed. Have these people come face to face with the miracle called Christ?

Between the hopeful and the fearful were others who did not approve but were not alarmed. Perhaps the German Christians were talking a lot of nonsense but there was always nonsense taught in other churches. Not everything was theology according to Karl Barth.

And Herr Hitler himself? What was his reaction to the German Christians?

Stewart W. Herman, pastor of the American Church in Berlin from 1934 until Pearl Harbor day, is of the opinion that Hitler spoke loosely, not realizing the full implications of the state-church relationship he sought. Writes Herman in his book, *It's Your Souls We Want:*

> Hitler's acquaintanceship with Christianity was confined to a sketchy childhood remembrance of Austrian Catholicism and to his political contact with nazified clergymen who led him to think that the German church could only be grateful to him for rescuing it from the clutches of atheistic bolshevism.

On April 3, 1933, the German Christians held a general conference in Berlin. They passed a resolution demanding that the church be *gleichgeschaltet* or coordinated with the state. They proposed a united Evangelical church with a

Reichsbishop at the head. It was to be a church bound up with the people (*Volk*), moreover, it was to maintain the purity of that people. There would be no mixing of races. Mixed marriages between Germans and Jews must be forbidden. Non-Aryans must be excluded from office.

The reply to this call to action by German Christians was a letter sent out to pastors by Dr. Otto Dibelius, general superintendent of Brandenburg, who wrote, "We are united in affirming that the Gospel stands in opposition to all human ideology, whether nationalist or socialist, liberal or conservative. The Gospel must not be subservient to the selfish wishes of men, but must be their judge."

And Niemoeller in his sermon on the fifth Sunday after Easter preached, "We cannot set up dividing walls within the community of Christ; we cannot enforce human claims within the community of Christ; we cannot cultivate fanaticism and passion within the community of Christ." Christianity, he added, would bear witness to God's grace by exercising love toward "all men and women, Christians, infidels, and Jews."

On April 26, 1933, an announcement suddenly appeared in the press. Hitler had appointed Military Chaplain Ludwig Mueller as his delegated authority and representative in all questions affecting the Protestant Church.

Mueller was an old friend of Hitler's. Aside from his dedication to National Socialism he had no qualifications for the position.

Martin Niemoeller has described Mueller as a "nationalist idealist, wanting things to work together without friction, a jovial, vain man who wanted to be somebody. He was no theologian; theology was at the brim of his hat."

The new Reichsbishop, called "Reibi," addressed a cordial appeal to all church members, inviting them to cooperate with the German Christians in building a real Reich church.

Early the next month the German Christians issued a statement of their program containing nine items. Among them was a Reich church of dominant Lutheran stamp, a church that recognized the authority of the National Socialist state, and a church of German Christians, "Christians of the Aryan race."

Meanwhile, the authorities of the Evangelical Church had not been idle. The Church Federation gave its president, Dr. Hermann Kapler, authority to carry out the reorganization of the church. He appointed a respected Lutheran leader, Bishop Marahrens of Hannover, and Dr. Hesse, Reformed pastor of Elberfeld, to meet with Mueller at the old Cistercian Monastery at Loccum. This conference of three was to come up with a recommendation for a Reichsbishop who would be accepted by all groups.

They came forth with a majority recommendation, a new nomination for Reichsbishop Dr. Friedrich von Bodelschwingh, Martin Niemoeller's old friend from Bethel, a popular and revered man whom no one could criticize. The church electors followed the instructions, and Von Bodelschwingh was elected.

Mueller quite plainly did not agree. In a radio address he protested that the electors had not "heard the voice of God," or they would have seen to it that their new leader came "from the ranks," the ranks of the German Christians.

Other German Christians took up the battle and started a shower of telegrams to Kapler, Von Hindenburg, and Hitler, demanding the appointment of Mueller as Reichsbishop. Matters reached a climax when the church synod met at Eisenach to appoint a successor to Kapler, who had resigned. Hitler intervened by appointing his own state commissioner, Dr. August Jaeger, who was "to bring order" into the church. Jaeger quickly brought his variety of order by dismissing opposition pastors right and left. Von Bodelschwingh resigned.

By June 30 things were in such a state of confusion that the aged Von Hindenburg reproved Hitler in an open letter, the first reprimand he had given his new chancellor. In it he referred to his "anxiety for the inner freedom of the church."

Nevertheless, by official ordinance, on July 2, the Nazi swastika flew over the churches and pastors were instructed to give thanks for recent developments and to ask divine blessing for the progress of the Nazi movement.

On July 7, it was announced that Mueller again would assume the title of Reichsbishop. However, since Nazi policy always demanded a show of legality, it was necessary that he be officially "elected." New elections were set for July 23.

The elections were a farce. All the power of propaganda was placed at the disposal of the German Christians. The press and radio were theirs exclusively. Hitler himself went on the air the night before the election and pleaded with the people to give unqualified support to his choice.

At the polls the next day, storm troopers were lined up at the doors. "Reibi" Mueller won an impressive victory.

A month later the new synod adopted the Aryan paragraph in which all persons "of non-Aryan descent" as well as those married to persons of "non-Aryan origin" were excluded from all offices of state. Marriage between Christian and Jew was prohibited, and persons of Jewish descent desiring to remain Christian would have to form themselves into special Jewish-Christian congregations and could not worship with other Christians.

Karl Barth in an essay, "Theological Existence Today," expressed the voices of the opposition, among them Martin Niemoeller's, when he wrote;

What I have to say to all this is simple: I say unconditionally and without reserve, "No" to both the spirit and the letter of this doctrine. I think that this doctrine is alien to the Evangelical Church. I think that the last hour of this church will have struck if this doctrine ever has sole sway within her, which is the object of the German Christians. I think that the Evangelical Church ought rather to become a tiny group and take refuge in the catacombs than under any circumstances make peace with this doctrine.

7.

"WE MUST OBEY GOD"

MARTIN NIEMOELLER's opposition group did not meet under the catacombs but they began meeting under the stairway. The parsonage on Cecilienallee became the scene in the fall of 1933 for evening gatherings. They were called Bible-study meetings but they were more than that. Eventually they were to combine religion, resistance, and reports of the latest news that Berliners could not get anywhere else.

"They began in a small way," Niemoeller described their origin. "I thought I might organize a club in my congregation to tell them about the basic credal foundations of the Protestant Church. I invited some people for an evening in our home. About twenty of them came to the first meeting."

Soon there were seventy, then a hundred, then two hundred. They filled the sitting room, the dining room, and the music alcove that looked out over the garden. Soon people were sitting on the curving stairs to the second floor. The children found it fascinating to peep out of their bedrooms and watch the crowds.

Soon there was not enough room in the house, so the meetings moved over to the Annenkirche. They quickly outgrew the little church, too, so they went across the street to the Gemeinde Haus, where the auditorium would seat eight hundred.

Part of Pastor Niemoeller's intention was to teach his

congregation more about the basic tenets of their religion so they would understand the principles of the conflict with the German Christians. He began by explaining the Augsburg Confession, then went through Luther's Small Catechism, page by page. The meetings still were being called "catechism evenings" long after they had left the catechism and were facing the cataclysm.

An American pastor, the Rev. Ewart Edmund Turner, clergyman at the American Church in Berlin from 1930 to 1934, attended these early meetings and has described them as "the first coals that started the fire of opposition."

"They were the first analysis of Hitlerism," he said. "The meetings were attended in great part by people who had thought the new government was going to be wonderful. They felt betrayed. Here was a man who said, 'Halt, we've got to review the situation.' They came to him as to a teacher.

"Two things were important about Niemoeller's position. One is that he was a nationalist, a super patriot, a war hero. Had he been a socialist or sympathetic to the Social Democratic party, as was Paul Tillich, his resistance would not have been so dramatic or important.

"Another important thing about Martin Niemoeller is that his resistance came early. Many people saw through Hitler four or five years later. Niemoeller's service was that, in spite of the mistakes he made before January, 1933, in analyzing Hitler, when he saw the direction in which the movement was going, he said no loudly and clearly."

By the middle of 1933 it had become plain that one of the directions of the new movement was toward the treatment of Jews as second-class citizens. Many of them had been dismissed from civil-service positions. Jewish doctors in hospitals, and professors in universities were summarily fired.

Soon after Reichsbishop Ludwig Mueller put into effect the

Aryan paragraph concerning Jewish-Christians, he demanded that every pastor sign an oath committing himself to the spiritual as well as the political leadership of Adolf Hitler. Martin Niemoeller's reply was the formation of a group of the clergy into the Pfarrer Notbund, or Pastors' Emergency League. By the end of August 2,000 pastors had joined. Its members declared:

(1) I pledge myself to fulfill the duties of my office as servant of the Gospel, solely according to the Holy Scriptures, and according to the confessions of the Reformation as the true interpretation of the Holy Scriptures.
(2) I pledge myself to protest, without regard to consequences, against every violation of such a confessional stand.
(3) I accept the friendly leadership and the mediating services of Dr. von Bodelschwingh in guarding against any infringement of such a confessional stand.
(4) According to the best of my ability I join in sharing the burden of those who are persecuted for making such a confessional stand.
(5) Conscious of this obligation, I bear witness that the application of the Aryan paragraphs to the life of the church is a violation of this confessional stand.

Nationalism continued its swaggering path. A new holiday was proposed, German Peasants' Day, to be celebrated around the time of the American Thanksgiving.

"Like the 'Day of German Labor' and 'Day of German Youth,'" Niemoeller preached in a sermon, "this might be a good and useful thing." But he warned, "This nation has not yet met again the living God." He warned that if disregard for God continued, "in the moment of supreme good fortune, God may stretch out his hand in anger against us; this lesson we learned from our nation's experience twenty years ago.

These were prophetic words. And yet many of his fellow clergymen felt that Martin Niemoeller was being a little hysterical when he warned of the dangers of worship of country.

Some of them reasoned that, after all, the founder of the Protestant Church, Martin Luther, had been a German. There was some basis for reveling in the German roots of their faith. Niemoeller warned against making a saint of Luther.

"There is absolutely no sense in talking of Luther and in celebrating Luther's memory within the Protestant Church," he preached on Reformation Day, "if we stop at Luther's image and do not look at Him whom Luther is pointing out to us. The temptation is great, for Luther as a German is nearer to us than the Jewish rabbi of Nazareth. Luther with all his corners and edges is less offensive to us than this Jesus whom—to our annoyance—no one could or can convict of sin. Between us and Luther the distance is relative, for when all is said and done, Luther is one of us; between us and Christ the distance is infinite, for after all Christ is God. But faith in Luther remains hollow and ineffective if we do not join with Luther in confessing our faith in Christ and Christ alone. Therefore I think that the best thing that has been said so far during the Luther jubilee is the simple message which Von Hindenburg gave to the present Reichsbishop: 'See that Christ is preached in Germany.' "

The Reichsbishop's answer to this impertinence was to send Niemoeller the first of many notices, suspending him from preaching. Niemoeller paid no attention to it.

In November, 1933, the German Christians held a mass meeting of 20,000 in the Sport Palace in Berlin. Dr. Reinhardt Krause, a high-school teacher and district leader of German Christians, delivered an appalling address which heaped scorn on the Old Testament and advocated a revision of the New, proposed that Germany rather than Palestine be the new Holy Land, and that the basis of a true *Volkskirche* be founded on the slogan, "One people, one Reich, one faith."

Said Dr. Krause:

"The first requirement is love of one's native land and the first step is to free the religious service and doctrine of everything un-German by the elimination of the Old Testament with its Jewish retribution morality and its stories of cattle dealers and concubines. This book has justly been characterized as one of the most questionable books of world history.

"It will also be necessary to exclude all reports of the New Testament, which are obviously misrepresentative and superstitious; also to exclude the whole scapegoat and inferiority theology of the Rabbi Paul, which was the beginning of the falsification of the Gospel message, 'Love thy neighbor as thyself,' or regard this neighbor as thy brother and God as thy father. It is very true that the whole course of development of dialectical theology from Paul to Barth has made our Father God into an intellectual chess game. Theology has always sought to separate God and man, always attempting to prove its own right to exist by viewing man laden with original sin, fallen, and therefore to be saved by the church. We know no separation of God and man unless man himself by his own will separates himself from God."

There was more of the same stamp. The speaker closed on a ringing note: "We reject the crucifix!"

A flood of protests followed the meeting. Martin and Wilhelm Niemoeller were among those who called on Reichsbishop Mueller. Up until this time Wilhelm's membership in the Nazi party had been pointed to by members of the resisting pastors as proof that they were loyal patriots but did not agree with what was being done in the churches. It was routine for them to say, "Why, we even have a member who wears the golden badge," meaning the golden badge of Nazi party membership.

But now Wilhelm tore up his membership card, threw it on the Reichsbishop's table and said, "I'm through."

Many others had the same reaction to the Sport Palace meeting, including some who had gone along with the German Christians but now had their eyes opened. On November 30 it was announced that Mueller's entire church cabinet had resigned. Mueller's consecration, to have taken place on Sunday, December 3, was indefinitely postponed.

Once again the Pastors' Emergency League met and drew up a statement of their convictions:

"We stand," they declared, "by the Scriptures of the Old and New Testaments, as the unique test of our faith and life and the Confessions of Faith as the reformed explanation thereof."

The phrase "Confessions of Faith" was the key. Theirs was not a national church, a German Christian church, a church of ritual and lip service. It was a confessing church—a *Bekenntnis-kirche*. This Confessing Church—sometimes termed the Confessional Church—was to grow in spirit and influence and make its resistance known in the struggle to come.

The German Christians rallied quickly from their setback. The Reichsbishop placed the entire group of Evangelical youth organizations, numbering 700,000, in the hands of the Reich youth leader, Baldur von Schirach, a follower of Alfred Rosenberg. The same was done to the Catholic youth despite the protests of Archbishop Faulhaber of Munich.

Dr. Wilhelm Frick, minister of the interior, ordered all newspapers and magazines, excepting specifically designated religious periodicals, to refrain from publishing religious news. The religious press itself was controlled and eventually wiped out of existence.

The effect of this ban on religious news was that many visitors to Germany were unaware that a church conflict was going on unless they happened to have close contact with certain members of the clergy. When the conflict was recognized by Nazi officials, they tried to make it seem a purely political fight among ecclesiastical factions for control of the new church government, "in which the government was acting only as a benevolent referee to prevent heads from being broken," as Stewart Herman describes it.

The fact that there were gradations of intensity of resistance among the Protestants makes it even more difficult for the impartial observer to assemble facts on the church struggle.

Michael Power likens the job of reporting the church struggle to that of a newspaper reporter trying to give a complete account of a boxing match with all its blow-by-blow changes, except that this was a "free-for-all in the course of which some of the contestants drop out and others appear to change sides." Probably the most detailed account in English is that of the dean of Chichester, A. S. Duncan-Jones, *The Struggle for Religious Freedom in Germany*.

Early in 1934 Mueller issued another edict designed to stop the pastoral resistance. Political discussions henceforth would no longer be permitted in the pulpit or in church buildings, and any pastor found guilty of attacking the church administration in speech or writing would be removed from office. If suspended, he would be deprived of pension rights.

On January 7, 1934, this decree was attacked from the pulpit by ninety-eight pastors of Berlin. On January 14 the same protest was read by pastors throughout the Reich. In part it read:

"Before God and this Christian congregation, we make complaint and protest that the Reichsbishop with his mandate of force threatens those who, for the sake of their conscience and of their congregation, cannot keep silent in the face of the present emergency in the church and of the laws newly passed contrary to our church confessions, which he had previously suspended for the pacification of the church.

"We declare that his contradictory conduct toward us makes it impossible for us to repose that confidence in him which he requires for his office. If we take a stand against his decree, we act according to the Augsburg Confession, in those articles which speak of the power of the bishops.

"We must also deal with the Reichsbishop according to the verse, *'We must obey God rather than man.'* "

8.

MEETING WITH HITLER

From the little town of Lippstadt on the Lippe River by way of Elberfeld, the Imperial Navy, and Muenster in Westphalia, came Martin Niemoeller. Adolf Hitler made his way from the mountainous regions of Austria by way of Vienna and the Munich beer halls. They met only once, but it was a momentous occasion.

It was in January, 1934, that the church dissension became so alarming that even the minister of the interior was concerned. An invitation went out for a group of Protestant churchmen to meet with the Fuehrer in his offices.

Niemoeller had great hopes for the meeting. According to Dr. Henry Smith Leiper, Niemoeller could not reconcile Hitler's actions to the high-sounding promises he had made before and immediately following his election. Leiper received a letter from a friend of Niemoeller, who wrote:

One who has listened to Niemoeller's sermons and speeches in parish meetings cannot doubt that he never got over his disappointment at having been betrayed, fooled by a promise which was broken immediately after having made so many loyal supporters for Hitler and his party. He was never oblivious to the fact that such support was born by false—deliberately false—pretenses.

Honest himself, Niemoeller could not conceive of such outright deception. He and others clung to the hope that perhaps there had been misunderstandings. Perhaps the Fuehrer had not been informed. Surely when he learned how far the German Christians had gone he would order them to stop.

Eight leaders of the opposition were invited to the meeting, which was set for January 25, 1934. They included Bishops Meiser, Wurm, and Marahrens of the older, more conservative group.

Just as he was about to leave his study for the meeting, Martin Niemoeller's phone rang. His assistant, a woman vicar, Christa Krause, told him it was Pastor Kuenneth, cochairman of the young Reform movement.

"Is everything all right?" Kuenneth asked.

Niemoeller said it was.

"I am at this very moment on my way to see Der Fuehrer," he explained.

Fräulein Krause felt the conversation was keeping the pastor from getting away on time so she took the telephone out of his hand.

"President von Hindenburg has been called to Herr Hitler's deathbed and Pastor Niemoeller is going to administer extreme unction," she joked. There was laughter from all three. Then Martin Niemoeller hurried outside and took a taxi into the city.

There were about forty people altogether at the meeting, most of them right-wing churchmen plus a few people who belonged to the Reichsbishop's office but were not in sympathy with the German Christian radical wing, and some of the German Christians themselves.

They stood in a half circle in Hitler's office waiting for him to enter. The Fuehrer came in and walked around the semi-circle and was introduced to each one in turn. Reichsbishop Mueller walked behind Hitler, and took his place by his side, but spoke to no one.

Hitler began to read a prepared address about the purpose

of the meeting but before he had covered more than a few sentences the door opened and Hermann Goering strode in. He put down his brief case, took out a piece of paper, and began to read.

"My Fuehrer," he said, "it is my painful duty to report to you that this morning Pastor Martin Niemoeller spoke on the telephone and discussed a plot against your life."

To say that Niemoeller was startled is to put it mildly. For a minute he could not recall any telephone conversation concerning Hitler. Then he remembered Fräulein Krause's quip.

The effect on Hitler was electrifying. He went into a tantrum and began to scream hysterically about the ingratitude of the Protestant clergy whom he had rescued from the clutches of marxism, and who were now determined to undermine his program by working behind his back.

"Do you think that by this backstairs politics," he demanded furiously, "you can drive a wedge between me and the president and injure the Third Reich?"

Niemoeller protested that they had no animosity toward the Third Reich, that their only concern was for "the German people."

"You leave the German people to me," screamed Hitler. "Look after your business of how to lead people to heaven."

"My Fuehrer," Goering again broke in, "I have definite information that the Notbund is supported by foreign powers."

Hitler cut him off wearily.

"There stands your Reichsbishop Mueller," he told the churchmen. "I did not elect him for you. It is your concern if you want to dismiss him. My only interest for the church is that there be peace."

He walked around the group again for his formal good-bys. When he came to Niemoeller, the pastor again spoke up.

"Herr Reichskanzler," he said, "the responsibility for our

German nation has been laid upon our souls and conscience by no earthly authority but by God himself, and no earthly authority can take away this responsibility from our hearts, not even you."

As they left the building, most of his fellow pastors ignored Niemoeller coldly. They seemed to take the attitude that the long-hoped-for meeting had gone wrong and it was his fault. His brashness and frankness—"Must you say it just that way, Martin?"— had ruined their chances for conciliation. Only one of them, Praeses Koch of Westphalia, came up to him and smiled.

"Now, Brother Niemoeller," he said, "we will have to go one flight higher." And he glanced significantly heavenward.

When Niemoeller returned home, Else met him at the door.

"Now, Martin," she said, "is Adolf Hitler a great man?"

"No," he said, "he is a coward."

He went on to tell her of Hitler's tantrum.

"When first he began shouting and raving," he related, "I prayed inwardly, 'Lord God, let him talk on and on until I know what to answer.'

"But the tantrum lasted so long, I was tempted to pray, 'Stop him.'

"Finally he did stop. He stopped when outside in the driveway a car drove up in front of the windows. The sound of the motor, the car door opening and closing, somehow broke into his subconscious. A certain look came over his face. He broke off and said, 'And every time I hear the sound of a car, I think here comes some idiot who is going to shoot me.'

"At that moment I got back my courage," Niemoeller told his wife. "For I suddenly had the feeling, 'Herr Hitler, you are haunted by fear. I fear, too, and I have reason to be afraid, but my fear is not as great as yours.' "

9.

CHURCH STRUGGLE BEGINS

In the early days of the Jewish persecution in Germany there was a popular anecdote in church circles. It told of an anti-Semitic pastor who stood before his congregation and said belligerently, "If there be a Jew in this house of God, let him get up and leave." No one stirred. No one spoke. But the crucifix over the altar slowly disappeared.

Entire books have been written on the subject of anti-Semitism in Germany. One can read statements substantiating carefully documented facts that no Germans were anti-Semitic. Or all Germans were anti-Semitic. That the Protestant Church's first protest against Hitler concerned anti-Semitism; that the Protestant Church secretly sympathized with anti-Semitism but objected to Hitler because he interfered with their own organization.

Not infrequently one hears, "Martin Niemoeller was as anti-Semitic as the rest of them. He was really a Nazi at heart."

What is the truth about Martin Niemoeller and the Jews?

One fact is this: In January, 1934, shortly after his meeting with Adolf Hitler, Niemoeller wrote a letter to his young non-Aryan friend Franz Hildebrandt in London, asking him to come back and help him in his work with the Pastors' Emergency League.

The son of a Lutheran father and a Jewish mother, Hildebrandt had followed his father's religion and studied for the ministry. He was a young curate in the parish of Machnow just west of Zehlendorf, near Dahlem, when he met Martin Niemoeller.

Although he had not yet reached the required age of twenty-five in June, 1933, he saw the handwriting on the wall concerning the Aryan paragraph then in dispute and he requested special permission to be ordained since he had the necessary credits. He was ordained on June 18 and a week later the church was in the hands of the Nazis. In November, 1933, he and a young friend named Dietrich Bonhoeffer left for England.

In January he received a letter from Niemoeller asking him to come back, or, rather, in typical Niemoeller fashion, telling him he should come back. He called the pastor from London to find out whether he was really needed. That was on a Saturday. On Monday he sailed.

Franz Hildebrandt is now a member of the faculty of Drew University, Madison, New Jersey. Asked for his opinion of Martin Niemoeller's sentiments toward the Jews in those Dahlem days, Professor Hildebrandt is quite frank.

"Martin Niemoeller was a member of the officers' class in which a certain amount of what my Jewish friends term 'Our dear old decent anti-Semitism' is almost taken for granted," he said. "You limit Jews in attendance at universities, you do not join the same clubs, your children do not marry them. Niemoeller may have condoned this kind of exclusion of Jews.

"*But*, when it became a question of treating Jews as second-class citizens, of taking their jobs, property, lives, he came to their defense and fearlessly so.

"In demanding that I come back and work closely with him, Martin Niemoeller showed his contempt for the anti-Semitic views of the Nazis."

Niemoeller had preached on the Sunday after the meeting

with Hitler. It was the Kaiser's birthday and a member of the Dahlem congregation, Freiherr von Sell, told Niemoeller that he was going to see the Kaiser that day and tell him what had happened. On Monday Von Sell returned with a gift. The Kaiser had sent Niemoeller a signed photograph of himself.

The following week Niemoeller received in the mail his second dismissal from office by the Reichsbishop. He respected this suspension and asked Franz Hildebrandt to preach in his place.

Most of the people of the congregation did not know Hildebrandt by sight and assumed that a substitute had been sent by the state, so they sat back, patiently awaiting a typical party-line sermon. Hildebrandt's first sentences electrified them. This was no Nazi.

The sermon made headlines in London. The London *Post* reported, "Fearless Attack on Hitler and Goering."

Hildebrandt was advised that it might be wise if he went to the Gestapo and complained about the inaccurate reporting in the foreign press. He did so, and then secretly informed their friends in London that they appreciated the publicity but not to overdo it.

In addition to the Niemoeller suspension there was another aftereffect of the Hitler meeting. The conservative Lutheran bishops, fearful that Niemoeller's words made it appear they were plotting against the regime, quickly issued a statement declaring their united and unshakable confidence in the Third Reich and their Fuehrer.

This surrender of the bishops was a great blow to the Pastors' Emergency League and a propaganda victory for the German Christians. By the end of February, seventy of the opposition pastors had been placed in "protective custody." On February 28 the German Christians held another mass meeting in the Sport Palace, at which Ludwig Mueller said:

"The time will come when only Nazis will conduct services and when only Nazis will occupy the pews. We want one people, one state, and one church."

Another repercussion was of a personal nature. The Niemoeller home was entered and searched and all papers pertaining to the Pastors' Emergency League were taken.

Exhausted by the events of the past few weeks, Pastor and Mrs. Niemoeller took a trip to Elberfeld for a rest. Franz Hildebrandt moved into their house to stay with the children.

At six o'clock on Sunday morning he was awakened by a terrible noise. The children were up instantly and they all ran downstairs. There they found a smoldering box of material placed next to the outside window by the front stairs. It had been a crude and amateurish attempt to bomb the house but it was so poorly done, it had resulted in nothing except noise and dust. Hildebrandt shuddered to think what would have happened had it been done properly.

He notified the Niemoellers of the incident and assured them the children were unharmed. Then he told the congregation at church that morning, adding the most interesting item of all—the fact that the police had arrived without being called.

The bombing had another effect on the Niemoellers. Their maid left them. Her parents did not want her to stay with a family that might be bombed any day.

The first synod of the *Bekenntniskirche*, the Confessing Church, met at Wuppertal-Barmen, May 29–31, 1934. Here representatives from all the Protestant churches found themselves at one. Their desire was not to found a new church or seek union, but to resist unanimously the destruction of the Confession of Faith. They declared:

In opposition to the attempts to unify the German Evangelical Church by means of false doctrine, by the use of force, and of insincere practices, the Confessional Synod declares:

"The Unity of the Evangelical Churches in Germany can only come into being from the Word of God in faith through the Holy Spirit. Only so does the church become renewed. . . .

"Do not let yourself be misled by frivolous speeches, pretending that we oppose the unity of the German people! Do not listen to the deceivers who twist our intention to make it seem that we want to rend the unity of the German Evangelical Church or to forsake the Confessions of our fathers!

"Try the spirits whether they are of God! Try also the words of the Confessional Synod of the German Evangelical Church to see whether they agree with the Holy Scriptures and with the Confessions of our fathers. If you find that we contradict Scripture, do not listen to us! But if you find that we are standing upon Scripture, then let no fear nor temptation keep you from traveling with us the way of faith and obedience to the Word of God, in order that God's people be of one mind on earth and that we in our faith experience that He himself has said, 'I shall not leave you nor forsake you.' Therefore, 'Fear not, little flock, for it is your Father's good pleasure to give you the kingdom.' "

The statement continued by declaring its steadfast acceptance of such biblical truths as, "I am the way, the truth, and the life. No man cometh unto the Father but by me." It rejected the false doctrine that "there are realms of our life in which we belong to Jesus Christ, but to other masters." It rejected the false doctrine "that the church is permitted to form its message or its order according to its own desire or according to prevailing philosophical or political convictions."

Its concluding Bible truths were, "Lo, I am with you always, even unto the end of the world," and "The Word of God is not bound." And the men who met there vowed that it would not be bound.

Another meeting was called at Barmen. United States church leader Henry Smith Leiper, who was a delegate as an executive of the Universal Christian Council, described it as "unforgettable."

"On the preceding day, in the home of one of the leaders of the opposition who was close to Niemoeller," he wrote, "I had met some of the storm troopers who were going out in uniform by motorcycle and motorcar to summon the synod, as post, telegraph, telephone were all under the watchful eye of the secret police and personal messages directly delivered were the only safe means of reaching the leaders of the opposition. These young lads were risking not only their political future but their civil freedom and possibly even their lives. But when the appointed hour arrived that dark and rainy Sunday afternoon, the big church in Barmen was filled to the last seat."

The bold declaration read there declared that the Reich church government was invalid and violated the laws of the church.

It concluded:

"Obedience to this church government is disobedience to God."

Upon the reading of the declaration, those prepared to approve it were asked to stand.

"The congregation rose as one man." Leiper reported, "and sang Luther's great hymn, 'A Mighty Fortress is Our God.' Their voices rang out strong and clear as they came to those words:

> "Let goods and kindred go,
> This mortal life also;
> The body they may kill;
> God's truth abideth still,
>   His kingdom is for ever."

These actions were not without peril for those who participated, and especially for Niemoeller in his position of leadership. In a sermon delivered on a Sunday in June, 1934, he referred to some of the war of nerves used against him.

"When it happens—as it did recently in our neighborhood," he said, "that members of the church attend divine services in order deliberately to leave the room very noisily during the reading of the scripture lesson and insult the preacher in the open street after the service, then the rift as it touches the church itself is merely becoming visible.

"I do not stand here as a prophet, dear brethren, or I should perhaps be obliged to paint a dark picture of the future— distress and tribulation coming upon the fellowship of Christ, lukewarmness and deflection in our ranks, with only a few of our number managing to save their bare lives and their bare faith."

Soon another incident arose to test Niemoeller's courage. The bloody purge of the Nazi party of June 30, 1934, took place. The people were told their Fuehrer had "put down a revolution," but the truth spread like wildfire. The following Sunday Pastor Niemoeller had to preach, and he wondered what to say.

"How can I tell them," he asked himself, "that Jesus Christ was raised from the dead and He is the master and that God's will is the highest will and authority, not the authority of Adolf Hitler when he commands people to be killed without cause, without law?"

That morning Martin Niemoeller walked up to the altar and instead of reading the Confession, he read the Ten Commandments. He paused significantly before he pronounced the commandment, "Thou shalt not kill." Then he paused again for twenty seconds. He continued to read the rest of the commandments, but everyone understood.

In August Mueller and Jaeger held another meeting in Berlin, at which an important new measure was passed, the law requiring clergymen to take an oath of allegiance to Hitler. The measure met with great opposition, even in the states of Wuerttemberg and Bavaria, the latter the birthplace and home of much of the Nazi movement. Of the 16,000 Evangelical ministers in Germany, 6,000 stood in their pulpits early in September and proclaimed their adherence to the "Confessional Union."

On September 23 Mueller's long-delayed consecration of office was held. Michael Power in *Religion in the Reich* says of the occasion, "Never before in history can the nominal head of a church have been solemnly invested with the trappings of his high office while the vast majority of his followers were gathering elsewhere praying that their church might be saved from his activities."

Mueller's consecration was actually an anticlimax. He had lost and was losing power. There were swastika flags and raised arms in the Protestant Cathedral in Berlin but no great crowds. Perhaps it was because it was a wet day. Or perhaps it was because the crowds were elsewhere. In Dahlem the church was filled to overflowing and many sang hymns in the rain outside.

New attacks were made on the church in Wuerttemberg where Bishop Wurm was placed under house arrest. In Bavaria, the church was cut in half. In Munich, Bishop Meiser was deposed, church papers seized, and things reached such a pitch that crowds gathered to protest the state's action. In a sermon Martin Niemoeller described it as "a reign of terror . . . being set up while the public is misled by lies and half-truths."

And in another sermon he said, "We see more and more clearly how there is being propagated a new paganism which wishes us to have nothing to do with the Saviour who was crucified for us, while the church which acknowledges the

Saviour as its only Lord is reproached with being an enemy of the state."

And again: "The devil is going about among us, trying to persuade us that the time of the church is past because the mighty ones of this world have withdrawn their favor from it. . . ."

And again: "The state has bluntly declared that Jesus Christ is not to be taken over into the new German faith."

The Confessing Church pastors were not alone in their criticism this time. A reaction began in the ranks of the German Christians themselves and it was rumored that Dr. Jaeger's resignation had been demanded. On October 20 the Confessing Church held its second synod in Dahlem and issued a message calling for a new church government and summoning the Council of Brethren to take over the leadership. Dr. Jaeger resigned. And on November 22 a provisional church government was established by the Confessionals, who asked that the official ministers support them.

They were moving boldly and swiftly. Perhaps they went too boldly and swiftly. At least there were some in the church who thought so. And here was where Niemoeller began to meet another enemy, not the enemy of the state, but the enemy within his own church.

Writes Hans Bernd Gisevius in *To the Bitter End*:

Niemoeller had to fight in two directions at once. First of all there were the Nazis. On the other hand he had to defend himself against those very people who stood closest to him and whose mode of reasoning was most akin to his. These people were the "patriots," those good Christians whose ideology stemmed from the days when "throne and altar" were one. They suffered most strongly from the chronic disease of German Protestantism, its unfortunate tendency to support faithfully any sort of government. They still tended to do so even when the Hitler dictatorship had become a grotesque mockery of all genuine authority.

Because of this, they were strongly moved by Niemoeller's anti-Nazi pleadings. But why must the man always be so incautious? Weren't things really "working out" at times even with regard to the church? It was necessary for Niemoeller to give this attitude serious consideration for he encountered it daily in his closest associates. He became familiar with a thousand variations of the "patriot" mentality. It is a bitter experience to find oneself at the decisive moment surrounded by hesitant, questioning, and frowning friends, or to be totally deserted by them.

The Nazis wanted to lock Christianity up in a ghetto and many Christians believed it was their duty to accept this isolation gladly. Niemoeller knew that it must not be accepted.

Gisevius answers the often-heard assertion that "Niemoeller had no political objections to the Nazis" thus:

"His stern rejection of National Socialism was in essence pure politics. The people who listened to him in his pulpit perfectly understood the practical conclusions implicit in his sermons. Hitler and Himmler knew this very well. They did not give a damn about religious questions. They knew perfectly that they were fighting Niemoeller on their own exclusively political plane. For this reason his arrest in the middle of 1937 had a significance that went far beyond the conflict of the church. To my mind, Niemoeller's incarceration removed the last personality around whom any sort of civilian revolt movement might have gathered.

"I still think Niemoeller was right in believing that the chance was worth the full devotion of his whole personality. Unfortunately, however, the number of his true adherents was too small."

Some were frightened, some were conservative, and believed one must be loyal to the government at any cost. And some felt that while there were abuses and excesses in the Nazi party, Martin Niemoeller was too blunt. When he said in anger,

10.

THE CONFESSING CHURCH

MARTIN NIEMOELLER liked to joke that his first book had been titled *Von U-boat zu Kanzel* (From U-boat to Pulpit) but that the next one no doubt would be *Von Kanzel zu Kittchen* (From Pulpit to Jail).

He was not the only one who made a play on the title of his autobiography. Some of the critics who felt this Westphalian was going through the wall instead of over it grumbled sourly that a better title for his memoirs would be *With U-boat to Pulpit*. He still retained too much of the militant air of authority to please them.

However, he had friends, loyal, good, close friends who felt that he was right all the way. There was Franz Hildebrandt, who was serving as treasurer of the Pastors' Emergency League. There was Pastor Heinz Kloppenburg and Praeses Koch, both of Westphalia; Pastor Wilhelm Jacobi who preached at the famous Kaiser Wilhelm Memorial Church, now a ruin, in Berlin; Heinrich Grueber and Hans Asmussen; Dr. Otto Dibelius; Pastors Elvartz and Vogel, and the young Dietrich Bonhoeffer, who had returned from England in 1935 and who was destined to become one of the martyrs.

They did not think that Martin Niemoeller went too far. Instead, they agreed with Martin Luther that "A twig can be cut with a bread knife but an oak calls for an ax." The drastic times called for equally drastic measures.

71

Not everything was grim and sober in the doings of these Confessing churchmen, courageous as they were. Martin Niemoeller, who is still boyish and full of fun and jokes, had a love of laughter then, too.

One of his favorite practical jokes was the telephone game which he and another pastor, Fritz Mueller—no relative of the Reichsbishop—loved to play. They would agree to confer on the telephone at a given time, perhaps 9 A.M. Then one would read names out of the telephone book at random to the other, in order to confuse the Gestapo.

When they heard the pencils scratching away, Pastor Niemoeller would stop and inquire solicitously, "Am I going too fast or shall I repeat?" And then he would spell or count out the misleading name and number.

The Gestapo often attended church services in civilian clothes, eager not to be recognized. But Pastor Niemoeller delighted in calling out loudly, "Give that Gestapo man a prayer book."

None of the controversy was kept from the pastor's family. Even the youngest of the children became familiar with the deficiencies of bishops and the skulduggery of party officials through their father's frank and fearless dinner-table conversation.

It was little Jochen who made the comment which has been quoted often: "It is terrifying that there are so few men of character in Germany."

"He had no secrets," Franz Hildebrandt has said of Niemoeller. "That was a part of his genius. Not many weeks before his arrest someone informed him that Kerrl planned a snap election to make the church a hundred per cent Nazi. While he respected his informant and did not name him, he immediately put in calls all over Germany to tell his friends, 'I have it on good authority that there is to be a special election and *I am going to tell my congregation. . . .*'"

This last familiar phrase, "I am going to tell my congregation," caused the Nazis to shudder. The one thing they did not want was that church difficulties should become public knowledge. Many a move was strategically blocked by Niemoeller's threat to bring the issue to the people.

His reputation, national and international, was growing that year of 1935. At the beginning of the year things had looked encouraging. Reichsbishop Ludwig Mueller seemed to be on the way out. But as A. S. Duncan-Jones described events:

"If the Reich Bishop had faded out, it by no means followed that his place was taken by the Provisional Church Government. They found themselves, indeed, faced more definitely by the naked power of the state, owing to the collapse of the smoke screen of a 'German-Christian' government."

The growing heathenism was noted in the press, the theaters, the schools. Over and over again the Old Testament was denounced as foreign propaganda and Paul dismissed as a "Jewish rabbi."

In March, 1935, five hundred pastors delivered a statement from the pulpit attacking the new paganism. Almost all were jailed or placed under house arrest. In Berlin forty of them, Niemoeller included, were taken to Moabit Prison. They were kept in a huge room which had only a few mattresses and most of them sat up all night. The next morning their jailers hastily set up forty cots and brought in mattresses and bedding. But at noon that day all but three of them were released. The three held over were Jacobi, Roerich, and Niemoeller.

That night the three of them sat together in the middle of the big room, surrounded by the empty cots.

It must have been a dramatic sight as Martin Niemoeller, silhouetted in the small circle of light cast by one bare bulb overhead, read to the two others in the big empty, dark room.

The scripture he chose was from the Book of Lamentations, chapter three, from which he read:

"It is good for a man that he bear the yoke in his youth.

"He sitteth alone and keepeth silence, because he hath borne it upon him.

"He putteth his mouth in the dust; if so be there may be hope.

"He giveth his cheek to him that smiteth him: he is filled full with reproach.

"For the Lord will not cast off for ever:

"But though he cause grief, yet will he have compassion according to the multitude of his mercies.

"For he doth not afflict willingly nor grieve the children of men."

The next day the three were released. And that same day Praeses Koch of Westphalia assured Minister Frick that "the statement will not be read by five hundred pastors from the pulpit next Sunday."

It was not; it was read by 1,500. More arrests continued. It became common practice to read from the pulpits the names of those pastors in prison. The tension, the divisions of sentiment continued. Even among those close to him opinion was sometimes divided as to whether or not Martin Niemoeller was wise in stirring up the opposition to the state.

One story illustrating the divided reactions has often been told by a friend of Niemoeller, Mrs. Marlene Maertens, widow of Admiral Erhard Maertens, a classmate of Niemoeller. The incident took place at the twenty-fifth reunion of his class at Kiel in May, 1935.

Niemoeller had preached a sermon in Berlin and then driven to Kiel for the last day of the Saturday-Sunday-Monday festivities. He had brought his son, Hermann, along to keep him from falling asleep at the wheel.

On Monday night there was a gala celebration at a yacht club. The women were in formal dress. There was champagne, dancing, gaiety. It was quite obvious that some of his old classmates sought out Martin Niemoeller while others ignored him.

He did not dance but sat at the side of the ballroom, occasionally smiling and waving to someone on the floor, but noticeably tired and subdued. Mrs. Maertens, sitting next to him, was silent for a while but finally burst out, "What is going to happen? How is all this going to end? Will the cause of Jesus Christ be victorious?"

His eyes lighted up, his famous smile flashed and his face fairly radiated the answer, as he asked, *"Zweifeln Sie etwa?"* which can best be translated by two words—"You doubt?"

At a meeting in June the controversy between the young reformers and the conservatives again flared up. Pastor Niemoeller and his associates by now were advocating a complete separation of church and state, even going so far as to declare that the ministry should depend upon voluntary contributions. In July the Lutheran conservatives met and created their own Lutheran Council, still a part of the Provisional Church administration but free to make other arrangements with the state if it chose.

As for the state, it was becoming more and more apparent that the support of fanatical Nazis was being given to the German faith movement. Hitler had decided to place Dr. Bernhard Rust in charge of relations between state and church, and Dr. Rust made it plain that the church must endorse nazism.

On July 19 the state announced the creation of the post of Reich Minister for Church Affairs, headed by Dr. Hans Kerrl. Again there was a move on the part of some of the clergy to come to terms with the state. The Pastors' Emergency League, sent out a letter on July 30 urging its members to stand firm. They pointed out that Kerrl's authority to "issue ordinances with binding legal force was in complete disregard of Hitler's promise in 1933."

Dr. Kerrl, in an effort to give an appearance of churchly form to his government, set up a central National Church Committee, headed by Dr. Zoellner, a distinguished, respected church leader, and the man who had given Niemoeller his first important post. He was admired by many, including the Confessional pastors. It was not easy for Niemoeller to disassociate himself from Zoellner's efforts to unify the church. His appointment had been a clever propaganda move on the part of the Nazis.

Yet [wrote Dr. Henry Smith Leiper] the younger man saw only too clearly how the older was being used by a crafty and designing government to woo where it had not been able to intimidate. . . . Because of that knowledge and despite all the personal costs involved, Niemoeller refused to have the confessional church organization go into the national or provincial committees Dr. Zoellner was setting up. His decision resulted in much misunderstanding, some bitterness, and a serious split among the opposition forces generally.

How right Niemoeller was in his judgment soon became evident. During the first months of 1936 the state endeavored to make a National Socialist "translation" of the Bible, omitting the law of Moses and identifying Jesus as a Galilean, not a Jew.

In January, 1936, Martin Niemoeller published a document which was to become famous in the church-state struggle, the *Kirchenkampf*, as churchmen call it. This was the pamphlet *Die Staatskirche Ist Da*—The State Church Has Arrived.

In it he pointed out through a series of carefully documented charges exactly how the church had become "an obedient tool in the hands of political power instead of proclaiming the

Gospel." It was, he added, "A church which nobody respects and which will perish from its inner lack of freedom."

A few months later the Confessing churchmen reached an important decision. They addressed a memorandum to Hitler himself. It was a private memorandum and all secrecy was used to avoid its being made public. In essence it asked two questions of Der Fuehrer: Did he or did he not wish to de-Christianize Germany? Did he or did he not wish to put himself in the place of God? The message pointed out that he had objected, a few years before, to the placing of his picture on church altars, but now he was being increasingly considered the mediator between God and the people.

They received no answer but the memorandum was made public. And a new wave of attacks on Christianity ensued, in schools, in camps, in public meetings. Not all churches all over Germany were drawn into the struggle. In some areas they were untouched—the "intact" churches, these were called—but in Prussia, in Niemoeller's territory, the arrests increased. More and more pastors were being supported by the free-will collections of the Confessing Church, while the Pastors' Emergency League endeavored through legal means to have the pastors reinstated.

Franz Hildebrandt, writing of this period, commented on the tremendous schedule Martin Niemoeller managed to carry. His day began with an early breakfast and confirmation classes at 8 A.M., for he continued to conduct these classes and the number of students increased rather than diminished. At 9 A.M. his secretary arrived for dictation, interrupted by numerous telephone calls and visitors. At midday there would be a session of the Confessing Church leaders, the Brethren Council, and quite often in the afternoon a wedding or a funeral, for his regular clerical services were in demand, not only in Dahlem but all over Berlin.

At 3 P.M. two days a week more confirmation classes were

held, and one evening each week the catechism classes for adults in the congregation. Meanwhile, Niemoeller preached, often at a different place every day. Hildebrandt summed it up. "There was never a time when he thoroughly relaxed."

Niemoeller was especially diligent in the conduct of the affairs of the Confessing Church. Pastor Heinz Kloppenburg, of Dortmund, Westphalia, has stressed the fact that Pastor Niemoeller insisted that their group meet as a legal body, not an informal society, so that their opinions would have greater force.

These meetings were held quite openly in the early days, in Dahlem or surrounding towns. But by 1936 and 1937 they were forced to go underground. There were two ways in which they managed to let their members know about the meetings. Either they received a card inviting them to have "coffee" on the occasion of "dear Anna's birthday," in which case the precise time and place were written openly on the card. The other method of notification was a printed announcement that the meeting would be held at a certain hour and a certain place, Wuerzburg time. This meant that the hour and the meeting place were correct but that the members should come twenty-four hours earlier.

Meetings were not always peaceful and harmonious. Niemoeller could be as outspoken with his friends as with his adversaries. Sometimes he would draft a sharp, forthright statement deemed too dangerous by his friends and they would rework it into something milder. On these occasions he would fume, fuss, threaten to withdraw, bang the door, leave the room.

This happened many times, and one day the committee, instead of following and placating him, let him leave and did not call him back. That night at the dinner table one of the children observed, "You'll have to invent something else, Vati. That doesn't work any more."

Then as now Martin Niemoeller was explosive but did not hold a grudge or let resentment rankle within him.

"I'm an old pacifist and I remember an argument we had about pacifism in which he took the other side," Franz Hildebrandt recalled about a Dahlem incident. "He insisted that the discussion go on even though he had to go and take a bath.

"We argued about many things but no clash ever became a personal issue. And you always knew when he disagreed. Another person might be a model of politeness but give you the feeling you would never be forgiven. His explosions would come quickly but go as quickly. He does not harbor bad feelings. He also does not have a grain of diplomacy, which is why he has never gotten along with politicians or hierarchies."

Pastor Niemoeller's bravery in the pulpit in those days has been recorded in the published volumes of his last sermons. Taken down in shorthand by a girl of Jewish descent, the last twenty-eight sermons he preached were smuggled to Switzerland, mimeographed there, and later published in book form under two titles, *The Gestapo Defied,* and *God Is My Fuehrer.* In these collections one gains a faithful picture of his courage.

On October 11, 1936, for example, he said, "The older children among you will know—and the younger ones will learn sooner or later—how difficult it is today to preach the Word of God, how it is mocked at and jeered at, how Luther is praised as a 'true German' but Jesus is sneered at.

"But Luther alone is nothing. Luther alone cannot help us any more than Frederick the Great can help us; but Jesus of Nazareth is the only one who can really help us. It is to Him that we may come with our questions and with our distress, with our pangs of conscience, with the sin and guilt which are undoubtedly present in our lives; we may come because the love of God has been revealed in Him."

And on November 8, 1936, he said:

"We love our nation: we must love it—we cannot and dare

not and must not do otherwise. But when things change so that the sword 'reaches into our soul,' when the Lord Jesus Christ calls, then we must tear ourselves free of the environment that has denied Him. Many a young Christian who has heard the Lord Jesus Christ being slandered in the training camp has refused to listen and said, 'I will go out and help Him to bear the cross and the shame.' And such young men have gone out and in so doing have given up their homes and the future, for their worldly prospects are finished."

In calling on all Christians to follow this single path he concluded:

"Dear friends, we will not look back, lay our hands in our laps and watch the de-Christianizing of our nation and see the Lord Jesus Christ depart while we merely sigh, 'What a pity.' We must follow Him and testify that we, too, are with Jesus of Nazareth and we know of no other kingdom but the kingdom of God."

It was small wonder that Dorothy Thompson wrote this tribute on August 26, 1936:

Socialists have fled abroad and outside Germany have voiced their protests or inside Germany have risked their lives by undercover agitation. Scientists have left Germany and so have artists and teachers. But no group of men of science, no academy of teachers or artists, no bar association, has risked concentration camp for scientific, academic, or artistic ideals. One group and one alone, inside Germany, has had the courage and the daring to attack fundamental theses of the totalitarian state and attack them openly, read them publicly, sign their names and give their addresses, in the face of the dictatorship and for Germany and all the world to see. That group is the pastors of the Confessional German Evangelical Church.

11.

"I MUST SPEAK OUT"

How long will he get away with it? This was the question Germans were asking each other. It was the spring of 1937, and the drama of state versus church, the swastika versus the cross was drawing to a climax. Far more intense than any theatrical pageant, this drama had an additional element of suspense, for the members of the audience were, themselves, participants. And no one knew how it was going to end.

In February, 1937, the attempts of the venerable Dr. Zoellner to pull the warring groups together fell through. The German Christians took control of the church in Luebeck, put nine Confessing pastors under arrest. Dr. Zoellner wrote a letter of protest and resigned.

"I have always admired your sincerity," Niemoeller told him. "Now is your chance; join the Confessing Church." Zoellner shook his head, but he was deeply touched, and on the day following his resignation he had tea with the Niemoellers. Brokenhearted over the turn of events, Dr. Zoellner lived only a few more months.

The conflict continued. The arrests, the searches, the cross-examinations before the Gestapo. On one occasion Pastor Niemoeller was conducting a funeral. Two plain-clothes men came to the chapel and followed him to the grave. When he had dismissed the congregation at the graveyard, they closed in on him.

"Come with us," they ordered.

"What shall I do with my car?" he asked with annoyance.

"I'll come with you," said one of the Gestapo men, "and he can follow us."

Mrs. Niemoeller went home with friends and Pastor Niemoeller got into his car, more than a little irritated. Always a driver who did not believe in wasting time when behind the wheel, he stepped on the gas, the car leaped forward, and rounded the first corner on two wheels. A gleam of deviltry came to his eyes as he noticed the Gestapo man pale visibly.

This was, of course, just one more skirmish in the war of nerves. He was questioned and released, another in the series of interrogations. The story about the wild ride that disturbed the member of the Gestapo was circulated, another in the list of stories that added to the growing legends about this man Niemoeller.

One popular story of the times concerned Von Ribbentrop, one of Hitler's chief lieutenants, who was serving as ambassador to England.

Von Ribbentrop had dropped out of church affairs in Germany but when he went to England he decided it might enhance his importance if he were a churchman, so he decided to rejoin the church. Inasmuch as his permanent residence was in Dahlem, he applied to Niemoeller for permission to re-enter the church.

When Niemoeller asked the routine question, "What is your reason for wishing to re-enter the church?" Von Ribbentrop replied simply, "Reasons of state."

"Insufficient reasons for joining the church," Niemoeller wrote, and returned the application.

People continued to flock to Niemoeller's sermons and public appearances.

"Get off here for Pastor Niemoeller," the conductor called as the *U-Bahn* neared the Jesus Christus Kirche in Dahlem.

At a meeting held in Frankfurt am Main in May thousands of people crowded the streets as they did when the Fuehrer spoke. But it was not for the Fuehrer. It was to hear the pastor from Dahlem, and the people were waiting for big St. Paul's Cathedral to empty so they could hear the service repeated.

Finally the church was emptied. The crowds, excited but orderly, filed in. Two other churches, connected by wire to St. Paul's, were just as crowded.

Pastor Niemoeller chose as his text the story of King Hezekiah, defender of God's city, Jerusalem. In the case of Hezekiah, he told the tense crowd, the enemy was known. The enemy was outside the city walls. Those who stood with Hezekiah, those willing to defend God's city, were inside.

"But we here," he said, "do not know the enemy. He may be sitting next to you."

In the church were storm troopers, *Junkers*, diplomats, bankers, as well as church members. No one dared look either right or left. As he closed, Niemoeller expressed his appreciation of the huge audience, then drove home his message:

"Do not come," he warned them, "to hear the famous Pastor Niemoeller. Come because you know that, as a nation, we are on the wrong way."

Does faith make martyrs or do martyrs build the faith? Certainly the Confessing Church was gaining inward unity despite the outward attacks. When the Prussian Confessional Synod met in Halle on the Saale, Niemoeller reported back to his congregation that "we have never had a synod at which we were inwardly so united or inwardly so near to each other in spite of the difficult problems and discussions."

On June 5 he again made one of his outward thrusts at the state:

"The Reich may last a thousand years," he quoted Hitler's

fondest boast. "To be optimistic about it, it may even last two thousand years, but it will not last eternally."

In the middle of June the Council of Brethren assembled secretly in Berlin. In the middle of their meeting they had to move to another location. They went to a church in the heart of Berlin, the Friedrichwerderschekirche.

While they were in session, the Gestapo entered and blocked the doors. Positive that he would be taken this time, Niemoeller hastily passed his diaries to Fritz Mueller. Under the business-like arrangement of the Confessing Church, when anyone was taken away a successor was ready to step into his place. But to his surprise, when Niemoeller stepped forward and identified himself, the Gestapo men nodded and went on to the next.

The following Sunday Martin Niemoeller preached again. It was June 19. The text was Matthew 5:13–16:

"Ye are the salt of the earth: but if the salt have lost his savour, wherewith shall it be salted? it is thenceforth good for nothing, but to be cast out, and to be trodden under foot of men.

"Ye are the light of the world. A city that is set on an hill cannot be hid.

"Neither do men light a candle, and put it under a bushel, but on a candlestick; and it giveth light unto all that are in the house.

"Let your light so shine forth before men," he concluded the familiar words, "that they may see your good works, and glorify your Father which is in heaven."

And then, with a heavy heart, Pastor Niemoeller read to the congregation the list of those who had been forbidden to speak or were evicted or arrested. Why had these people been imprisoned? Because they claimed the church had the right to denounce attacks against the Christian faith freely and publicly, to denounce the decline from Christian faith openly, and to denounce interference with Christian worship fearlessly. The Fuehrer had given his "word of honor" to the church that it could defend itself.

"Now," demanded Niemoeller, "does the Fuehrer's word still hold good?"

And how could the Christian interpret God's word in the light of present-day happenings? What did it mean to say "Ye are the salt of the earth"? What was meant by saying that Christians must not allow the salt to lose its savor?

It meant, he said—and here the fire in his voice began to return—that the Gospel must remain the Gospel, the church must remain the church.

"And we must not—for Heaven's sake—make a German Gospel out of the Gospel; we must not—for Heaven's sake—make a German church out of Christ's church; we must not —for God's sake—make German Christians out of Evangelical Christians."

To continue with the message, what was meant by the sentence "Neither do men light a candle, and put it under a bushel, but on a candlestick; and it giveth light unto all that are in the house"? Did it mean to protect the candle from the wind?

"When I read out the names a little while ago," he said, "did we not think: 'Alas and alack, will this wind, this storm, that is going through the world just now, not blow out the Gospel candle? We must therefore take the message in out of the storm and put it in a safe nook.'"

That was not meant at all. The Lord Jesus Christ had not given us the candle to protect it from the wind.

"Away with the bushel." Niemoeller thundered. "The light should be placed upon a candlestick! It is not your business to worry about whether the light is extinguished or not by the draught . . . we are only to see that the light is not hidden away—hidden away perhaps with a noble intent, so that we

may bring it out again in calmer times—no: 'Let your light
so shine before men. . . .'

"It is a strange pass to which we have been brought today,"
he continued reflectively. "It has come to this: we are being
accosted on all sides by statesmen as well as by the men on the
street, who tell us: 'For God's sake, do not speak so loudly or
you will land in prison. Pray do not speak so plainly; surely
you can also say all that in a more obscure fashion!' Brothers
and sisters, we are *not allowed* to put our light under a bushel;
if we do so, we are disobedient; we have received our com-
mission from Him who is the light of the world. He does not
need us as wicks. He can take other wicks as well, other men
on whom He can set up His light as on a candlestick.

"Surely the practical meaning of this is: I must speak thus
once again today, for perhaps I shall no longer be able to do
so next Sunday; I have to tell you that today once again as
plainly as I can, for who knows what next Sunday may bring
forth?"

The words were prophetic. The next week brought forth
much. On June 22 Joseph Paul Goebbels spoke in Olympic
Stadium in Berlin. Huge bonfires burned at each end of the
arena where Italian Ballila, youthful Fascists, Hitler's storm
troopers, and costumed folk dancers participated in a festival.
The theme of Goebbels' discourse was, "The new era cannot
be held back—the old days are gone forever." And of the
church conflict:

"National Socialism has no desire to establish a new church.
We have enough churches in Germany already—indeed,"
with heavy sarcasm, "sometimes it looks as though we have
too many." To those who viewed Germany as an unhappy
land torn by religious strife, Goebbels assured them "all
Germany is happy except a few hundred preachers and sexual
criminals who are out of luck. . . .

"We don't want church strife—but in this Germany down

here on earth it is we who govern and every German must obey our laws."

On Wednesday eight members of the Council of Brethren were arrested. On Friday night three secret policemen attended evening communion at Jesus Christus. On Saturday, at Saarbrücken, six women and one man were taken into custody for distributing election leaflets of the Confessing Church. On Sunday morning the historic Annenkirche was closed because Pastor Fritz Mueller and forty-seven others had been taken into custody. And Pastor Niemoeller took this occasion to tell the story of Gamaliel, the lawyer, whose intercession had permitted the Apostles to continue their work, even though they had declared openly: "We ought to obey God rather than men."

"It was a moment critical beyond measure in the life of the church," said Niemoeller. "The Apostles had violated the injunction to silence which the authorities had laid upon them."

The message was plain:

"Our duty must be that of the Apostles: to go forth and preach the Word. For man does not live by bread alone, but by the Word of God.

" 'If any man will come after Me, let him deny himself and take up his cross—daily—and follow Me,' " quoted Niemoeller, then added, "It may be a good thing that this is no pleasure excursion and that the way of the Cross cannot be learned overnight. It may be just as well that the road is long and difficult, otherwise we might confuse our pious moods, our loyalty to our convictions, our manly courage, and whatever else the idols may be called, with faith."

That was Sunday, June 27. On Monday Niemoeller visited Professor Richter, the theological professor for mission work at Berlin University who was entertaining a group of religious visitors. Hans Lilje, Otto Dibelius, and Martin Niemoeller addressed the group. Niemoeller began by speaking in German but the English translation did not please him so he switched to English.

That evening there was a big open meeting at the church. The Gestapo came in and confiscated the collection. The next morning Niemoeller left for Wiesbaden to give some addresses there. The next compartment was filled with plain-clothes men.

He spoke at an early evening service in Wiesbaden's Marktkirche, later at a second one. Then the Confessing pastors met in a special room at the railroad station.

Here Martin Niemoeller had to decide whether to go back to Berlin or go to Bielefeld as Pastor von Bodelschwingh had urged him to do in a telegram. He decided on Bielefeld, took a midnight train for Cologne, and continued on to Bielefeld.

The meeting the next day lasted until 5 P.M. Niemoeller took the 6 P.M. fast train to Berlin and was home by midnight. He asked an assistant to take the morning confirmation class so he could sleep late. "Late" for Martin Niemoeller is not really very late. He was down to breakfast at eight thirty.

The house was less hectic than usual. Hermann, Jochen, and a friend had taken a train that morning to visit friends. Jan had stayed behind because he was sick. Brigitte was there, but Hertha and Jutta were also on a vacation trip. A group of pastors were conferring with Franz Hildebrandt in another room. The baby Tini (young Martin), not yet two, was toddling around.

"I think I'll take little Martin and go for a walk," Pastor Niemoeller said.

Just then the bell rang.

Eight Gestapo men pushed their way in.

"This is a private house," one of the pastors protested.

"There are no private houses in the Third Reich," said one of the Gestapo men.

"Pastor Niemoeller, come with us," they ordered. "We want to question you. You will be back soon."

Martin Niemoeller went with them as he had before on similar orders. But this time he did not come back. Not for eight years.

12.

THE MOCK TRIAL

Those members of the family and persons visiting in the house at the time were held prisoner all day. Among them were eight pastors who were having an early-morning meeting. Mrs. Niemoeller was glad they were there. It gave her and Fräulein Dora something to do, preparing meals for the group.

Brigitte, the seventeen-year-old, tried to telephone to friends to notify them of her father's arrest, but the lines had been cut. She managed to slip out of the house, climb the fence at the back of the garden, and get her message through.

Jan, who was twelve years old, was the only child, besides Brigitte and the baby Tini, who was at home. He sat at the piano most of the day, playing hymns, the only thing he could think of to do in order to comfort his mother.

Hermann and Jochen were visiting in East Prussia at the estate of a baron who had been friendly to their father. When news reached him, the baron called them in and said, "Well, boys, I have sad news for you. Your father has been arrested." The boys stood in silence for a moment, then returned to their play. The idea of their father being in jail was an old story to them.

The Gestapo returned to search for collections from the Confessing Church. After several vain attempts, they located the hiding place, a safe behind a picture, and took money, jewelry, and all the records of the church.

That evening the eight pastors were allowed to leave. A group of girls from the church came over and sang beneath the windows, another gesture of consolation for Mrs. Niemoeller.

As for the pastor himself, his reaction to the arrest was a simple one. His first thought was, "Thank God, now I can sleep." All the responsibility, all the tension, all the anxiety of the past few months fell from him and he collapsed from sheer exhaustion in his cell at Moabit Prison.

This did not last very long. Martin Niemoeller is not a man to enjoy a prolonged period of enforced rest. He was soon eager to plan for his trial and eventual release.

He was told the trial would be held in four weeks. Then it was postponed. He paced up and down his cell and utilized his energy in writing letters.

At first he was allowed to receive and answer as many letters as he wanted, but so many poured in that he was restricted to writing twelve post cards a day. Diligently he wrote exactly twelve each day. This was his "congregation," he told himself. He would continue to preach the Word of God to them. The post cards contained Bible verses, messages, sermons in miniature. Even today, when he tours the world, Niemoeller occasionally meets someone who shows him one of those tattered post cards, treasured all these years.

Shortly after his imprisonment, an intercession service was held at the Jesus Christus Church, but the crowd found themselves locked out by the Gestapo. They formed a procession, 250 of them, singing "A Mighty Fortress Is Our God" as they walked through the Schwarzegrund parklike area to the Annenkirche in Dahlem Dorf. When they arrived at the little church, they found it, too, had been locked, and the Gestapo were still there. All 250 were taken prisoner, plus a few pro-testing passers-by who knew nothing about the service.

Franz Hildebrandt, who had stepped into Niemoeller's place, thought he saw the handwriting on the wall and made his plans for escape. He and Niemoeller had intended going to the Oxford Faith and Order Conference in England in July but Niemoeller's passport had been withdrawn just before his arrest. Hildebrandt's was still in order and he decided to go, as if for a visit, but not to return.

Fortunately he did not have his passport with him on the Sunday he preached his last sermon for he was arrested—not because he was suspected but because they had taken up a free-will offering for the Confessing Church. After four weeks in prison, he was able to get away to Switzerland and then to England. There he was active in keeping Niemoeller's name before the public as part of the plan that the pastor must not be forgotten or allowed to disappear from the public con-sciousness.

All these efforts on the part of friends helped Niemoeller's cause psychologically, but they did not help him to be brought to trial. He did not suffer any discomfort. His cell was adequate. His wife was permitted to order meals for him from a nearby restaurant, for which he had to pay. He could be visited by Else in company with one or two of the children and they were a great source of consolation to him, especially Jochen, whom his father called "the pastor's pastor." And little Jan who, when asked by a guard, "Do you know why your father is in prison?" replied, "Yes, for preaching the truth of the gospel."

But none of this aided in his release. He was left to write his post cards, to look at the pair of falcons (an odd sight in the heart of Berlin) on a high chimney which he could see from his window, to read his Bible, and pray.

At last the trial was set for February 8, 1938. Dr. Carl

Schneider, American church historian, was in Berlin at the time and described to friends at home the public interest and excitement over the trial. He thought he could gain admittance by arriving two hours before the doors opened but found a big crowd already on the scene. When the doors did open, the early arrivals rushed up the stairs, but by the time the last ones had started up, the first ones were on their way down. The order had been given that no one would be permitted to view the trial. Even Mrs. Niemoeller was barred after the opening procedure.

Only twenty-eight representatives of various government offices were permitted to remain together with a small committee of Confessing Church clergymen. The charge was sedition.

The opening was delayed by defense protests against the secrecy. Then the trial proceeded, the defense bringing forth testimony to the effect that Martin Niemoeller had been an ardent patriot, that he had served during World War I, had fought against the Spartacists, had voted for the Nazi ticket in 1924. Three Confessing Church witnesses were allowed to testify along with a number of army officers and members of his congregation.

On the second day the Confessing Church members were barred. Niemoeller reacted by dismissing his three attorneys. If he were to be tried in secret, he said, he would act as Jesus had before Pilate, and make no reply to the accusations. He returned to his cell for ten days, and refused to talk with the official counsel of defense who called on him.

The judges and the authorities behind the scene tried to reach a compromise, which would allow one Confessing Church witness to be present. After a two-week interlude the trial began again.

On March 2 the trial was concluded. The accusation of high treason had been dropped and Niemoeller was convicted only of abuse of the pulpit for political ends, and sentenced to seven months' imprisonment. Since he had already served eight months, the sentence was considered to have been carried out.

The trial was over at noon, but the pastor stayed on to talk to his lawyers that afternoon. Dr. Hans Bernd Gisevius took Mrs. Niemoeller to lunch at a nearby café. During the luncheon he excused himself and went to the telephone to talk to friends in the government. When he came back, he broke the news to her gently. Her husband would not be released as they had been told.

The judges had recommended that he be released, but the Fuehrer would not hear of it. When the minister of justice had protested that there were no legal grounds on which Niemoeller could be held, Hitler interrupted him.

"In that case," he said, "he shall be my personal prisoner."

That night, the night of March 2, 1938, Niemoeller was taken to Sachsenhausen concentration camp in a limousine. He was registered at the office. His weight—one hundred forty six German pounds—was recorded. His picture was taken—front view, right side, left side. All of his possessions were removed, his Bible, wallet, papers, wedding ring, all the things that had been returned to him when he left Moabit.

Then he was led through a big iron gate into the camp. The camp was not encircled by a wall at that time, as it was later, but only by electrified barbed wire. Later on this was replaced by spiked walls and barbed wire.

He was led through a second iron gate, into a special compound, and through an iron door into a long, low brick building, a bunker consisting of sixty to seventy-five cells. All of these had iron doors. He was taken to cell number one and there he was left to himself.

"That night I was very cross with God," he has often said. "I did not sleep for a moment although I had never suffered from insomnia. I was angry, not because they had taken away my wedding ring and my wrist watch but because they had taken away my Bible.

"I did not sleep a moment that night."

The next morning he was led by a guard to the toilet and washroom. It was a general room for the use of all the prisoners in that area but he was always taken there by himself, never with anyone else. Then he was brought back to his cell. A broom was put in the cell and he was told to sweep the floor and clean the room. After a while another prisoner, an orderly, came to take the broom away.

He stepped off the room to measure its size. It was seven steps long and four steps wide. It had a cot with a mattress, placed on wooden planks, not springs. There was a blanket and a straw-filled pillow. There was a shelf with a cup for water, and a water tap and a toilet in the corner. A table shelf, which could be clipped down in place, a footstool, and a chair without a back comprised the furnishings.

The window was lower than it had been in his cell at Moabit. He could stand on the stool and manage to peer out.

He was not alone long that first morning. The commandant of the camp, an SS officer with the rank of major, came in, accompanied by a guard.

"You are Pastor Niemoeller," the officer said. "You have been brought here as a special prisoner. There is no such category and I do not know how to treat you. Do you have any wishes or complaints?"

Pastor Niemoeller took a deep breath and drew himself up to his fullest height.

"Last night," he said icily, "when I was brought here, your guards took away everything, my wedding ring, my wrist watch, my wallet, and a book that I treasure above all else and which I was allowed to have at Moabit, namely my pocket

Bible. If you ask me what I want, I want my Bible, and that immediately."

The commandant looked nonplused. There was nothing in the rule book to cover this situation. Bibles were not permitted in concentration camp cells but on the other hand he had no special instructions as to how this special prisoner should be treated. After a few moments of inward debate he turned to the guard.

"Go to my desk," he said. "His Bible is there. Bring it to me."

Often in the days after he had been released from concentration camp Martin Niemoeller told this story, and he liked to end it triumphantly with these words:

"I had been in concentration camp ten hours and I saw the power which belongs to Jesus Christ and not to him who imagines that he has power. Jesus Christ can enter through barbed wire, and iron gates, and consecutive iron doors, over and against the orders of a Fuehrer."

13.

BEHIND PRISON DOORS

WHEN asked the familiar question, "How did they treat you in concentration camp?" Martin Niemoeller is likely to retort rather sharply, "They didn't treat me. They left me alone."

More misconceptions and misrepresentations have appeared and been repeated about this phase of Niemoeller's life than any other. On the one hand, it has been said that he was "Hitler's special prisoner"—which he was—and that as such he received special privileges and was housed in luxury and comfort, somewhat like an upper-bracket income-tax evader.

On the other hand, stories appeared during his imprisonment that described how he was brutally beaten, how he crept among the dead and dying, ministering and praying with them. A book entitled, *I was in Hell with Niemoeller,* by a refugee, Leo Stein, gave a graphic account of the horrors which the author said he had seen Niemoeller experience in Sachsenhausen. This book, which appeared while Niemoeller was in prison, also quoted him at great length on his life just before his arrest and the events of the church struggle that led to imprisonment.

Pastor Niemoeller finds no fault with the accuracy of the statements concerning the church struggle or many of his own views. However, to the best of his recollection, he says he first met the author in 1947 after the war was over, and that he does not remember any contacts with him in prison.

It seems unlikely to Martin Niemoeller that an eyewitness account of his time at Sashsenhausen could have been written for the simple reason that there were almost no eyewitnesses to his daily life. He was in solitary confinement for his entire two years there.

On the same morning that his Bible was restored to him he was taken to be outfitted in prison clothing, striped pants and a jacket in a greenish-blue and gray. The tailor, also a prisoner, stitched a red triangle to his jacket. This meant that Niemoeller was a political prisoner. Jews were designated by yellow triangles, professional criminals by green, homosexuals by violet.

Over the triangle the tailor put a white stripe with a printed number, 569. This was Niemoeller's first prison number. Within six months it was changed to 10506. When he went to Dachau, he became 26679. The numbers themselves tell a story.

In the study of Niemoeller's Wiesbaden home is a cigarette box made for him as a gift by a prisoner he met at Dachau, a Polish count, Alexander Zamoyski. On the box is engraved 1937—1944, because at the time they optimistically expected to be released in 1944. Along with the dates are the three prison numbers. It is still disquieting to Niemoeller to look at those numbers. Psychologically they bothered him.

"I remember the feeling when I first saw the number," he has recalled. "I thought, 'You are not worth anything any more. There is a registry with this number written in ink and alongside it is your name written in lead pencil, so that when you die, your name may be easily erased and your number then gets another man.' "

After this first day of human contact he was left alone. He could read. He could pray. He could walk up and down.

But the only man he saw was the orderly who brought him his meals and the cleaning implements to straighten up his room. It was monotonous, it was maddening.

Martin Niemoeller has often said that he was not beaten, was not physically tortured in concentration camp. The point cannot be made strongly enough that for a man of his temperament, voluble, outgoing, accustomed to human contacts, human relationships, to talking things out with anyone and everyone, this solitary confinement was worse torture than the rack.

After three months he was led by guards one day to an automobile and taken, without explanation, to the police station in Berlin. Here he was allowed to have his first visit with his wife. These visits were permitted at irregular intervals and they were the pastor's only contact with the outside world, his sole hope.

They were allowed to talk only about the children, but with seven children one does not run out of conversational material, and Else Niemoeller did her best to save up the funny stories, the bright and amusing anecdotes. One of these told about a pastor visiting in their home who was enumerating some of the infamous criminals who were housed at Sachsenhausen, when one of the little boys inquired innocently, "Mother, are there bad people in prison, too?"

Sometimes Else was permitted to bring one or two of the children and occasionally brother Wilhelm accompanied her. Despite the sharp eyes of the guards, they managed to exchange some news besides that of strictly domestic matters. Martin Niemoeller learned, for example, of the services of intercession that were being held for him in Germany and in England. He learned of the groups that were praying for him; he has often been called "the most-prayed-for man in history."

Not only religious groups but many others were concerned about him. Miners and farmers sent delegations to Adolf

Hitler to protest his continued imprisonment. Some of them spoke out sharply against the persecution of religion. Said one Westphalia miner at a protest meeting, "I have the lung disease that we all die of. My father died of it. His father died of it. My son has just entered the mines. If you radical fellows take our Christ away from us miners, what have we got left?"

This public concern over Martin Niemoeller undoubtedly had its effect on his treatment. After the war was over, when Alfred Rosenberg's official papers were made public, it was learned that at one point in 1938 death was decreed for Martin Niemoeller, but the decree was rescinded because it was considered too risky to do away with such a popular figure.

He remained in his cell, like a potato rotting in a bin. He was permitted to write two letters a month, and these were some release for him but such release did not come often. He sank into the depths of despair.

The food was poor in this early period of his imprisonment. It consisted of potatoes that had been frozen and were inedible, a gray, moist, heavy bread, and coffee the equivalent of colored water. He felt sick most of the time. His eyesight began to fail him.

One day at the dinner table Else Niemoeller unburdened herself to the children. She was worried about Father; he looked so thin, he had so little to eat. Hertha and Jutta talked about it at school. It impressed one of their girl friends. In childlike fashion she sat down and wrote a letter to Adolf Hitler.

"Dear Fuehrer," the letter read, "the father of my friend is so ill. He has nothing but bread and water to eat. Can't you liberate him?"

Else Niemoeller was called to the Gestapo office and roundly scolded.

"You are telling people that Pastor Niemoeller lives on

bread and water," they said to her. "That is not true. You must stop circulating such lies."

She did not answer. But from then on, the food improved. The change came on Christmas Day, and Niemoeller was under the impression that he was being given a holiday treat.

"What's the matter? Didn't you have any appetite that you are bringing your dinner to me?" he joked with the guard.

But the guard said, "No, no, this comes to you under orders."

Care was taken that there be no unnecessary unrest among a people being readied for an all-out war. From then on Mrs. Niemoeller realized that one could accomplish more indirectly than directly. When the pastor's eyes troubled him she said artlessly over the telephone to a friend, "My husband's eyes are so bad. I am sure he will become blind." Almost immediately she was notified by the Gestapo that her husband had been taken to an eye specialist, and on another occasion to a dentist.

Not infrequently, when Else Niemoeller went to the police station to see her husband, she sat in the waiting room with women in mourning who had come to receive the urns containing the ashes of their dead. And the chill, the inevitable question would occur to her: "When will it be my turn?"

She would return home from these visits distressed, disturbed, grateful for the complexities of the household that took her mind off her troubles.

A great source of comfort to her during this time was Dora Schultz, her housekeeper, Fräulein Dora to friends, Tante Dora to the children, Doerchen to the family.

"I always say I'm married twice, once to my husband, and once to Dora," Mrs. Niemoeller has often said.

Less than five feet tall, less than one hundred pounds in weight, Fräulien Dora is little in size but mighty in spirit. When she was first sent to apply for a job in their household in 1936, Dora was almost rejected because Mrs. Niemoeller considered her too frail-looking. However because there was another maid, Grete Zachary, she took Dora on to share the work.

Grete left and Dora stayed, a tower of strength in those difficult days. Not only was she efficient and calm but she possessed that kind of contempt for officious authority and pomp which the Niemoellers appreciated, and spunk enough to live up to her feelings.

Once when the Gestapo came to the house for another search, Dora opened the door a crack and said sharply, "You can't come in now, Mrs. Niemoeller is taking a nap. You must come back later." And they did.

On another occasion Pastor Helmut Gollwitzer had been collecting clothing for Jews and storing it in the Niemoeller home. The Gestapo heard that something was being collected but had the erroneous impression that it was food. They came to the house and demanded to see the storeroom.

Often the Niemoellers did have extra food, thanks to the kindness of parishioners and sympathizers. Following the pastor's arrest, an anonymous donor left a goose tied to their door each Sunday for five weeks. When Mrs. Niemoeller gave the fifth one to someone she thought was hungrier, one of the boys said, "Thank goodness, we don't have to eat goose again."

But on this occasion there were no gift packages of food stored away, no surplus, only a large supply of several dozen chocolate bars saved to take the pastor in prison.

"I have nothing on hand," she told the Gestapo. "Just some chocolate I've been saving for my husband." But she felt uneasy when she thought just how much chocolate she had.

The Gestapo went through the house, leaving the kitchen until last. When they went upstairs, Mrs. Niemoeller made a sign for Dora to go to the kitchen. She started out the door.

"Stay here," ordered the Gestapo.

Dora slipped by nimbly. "I take orders only from Mrs. Niemoeller," she said.

When the search party reached the kitchen, Mrs. Niemoeller opened the pantry door reluctantly. There were five lone chocolate bars on the shelf. She looked at Dora. Dora did not change expression. When the men started to leave, Dora had the last word.

"How could we save food in this household," she asked, "with twelve hungry people and everything rationed?"

The Gestapo men opened the front door. Then one of them turned and whispered to Mrs. Niemoeller confidentially, "How is your husband? Can you tell us, is he getting along all right?"

In 1939 Else Niemoeller was permitted to go to Sachsenhausen to visit rather than climb the dirty, ugly dark stairs of the police station and wait with those who were there to receive urns of ashes. Sachsenhausen was a lovely place on the outside, with its flower beds and a pond with two swans swimming on it.

"Those poor swans," she often thought. "What things they must see."

A saving factor for Martin Niemoeller's sanity was his "congregation" in Sachsenhausen. For despite solitary confinement and walls and barriers, he managed to preach the Word of God to other prisoners.

For example, one day he climbed on his footstool and peered through the chinklike opening into the cell next to his and found a new occupant there. It was Ernst Koenigs, a pastor with whom he had gone to school in Elberfeld.

From that day on, whenever Niemoeller was permitted to take his twenty-minute walk in the courtyard—still in solitary —he slowed down as he passed under the window of his friend and called out the gospel and the epistle lesson for that Sunday. On one side of the court was the barbed-wire fence and above him a watchtower with a guard scrutinizing everything that went on. He became adept at speaking swiftly out of the corner of his mouth.

When other prisoners walked in the courtyard and he was confined to his cell, he would stand on the footstool and in a loud voice recite verses from the Bible.

He learned that the gardener who tended the beautiful flowers that Else admired was a Catholic priest, a teacher from Bavaria. Through the orderly Niemoeller obtained a Roman Catholic missal and undertook to read mass to the priest as he worked outside the window. He studied the book carefully so he would be sure to have the right mass for the right day.

There are those who say it was this act of reading mass through his window that gave rise to the rumor that Martin Niemoeller had become converted to the Roman Catholic faith.

The truth is that while Martin Niemoeller did not become a convert to Catholicism, he did study the religion and gave serious thought to conversion. He was discouraged when he heard that many of the clergy in his own church were half-hearted in their stand against the state, were fearfully compromising, and "going along." The Roman Catholic Church seemed, as he later described it, "like something solid and clear cut."

He talked over his doubts and indecisions with his wife. It was a close friend, Father Gebhardt, of the Catholic church in Dahlem, who urged Mrs. Niemoeller not to encourage her husband to change his faith under the duress of prison but to wait for calmer times.

Later on, in Dachau, Martin Niemoeller reached the conclusion that the Catholic faith was not the answer for him.

But he has never denied that he considered it in all seriousness.

His consideration of conversion was one of the rumors that was hotly debated during his imprisonment in Sachsenhausen. Another action that aroused attention and controversy took place in September, 1939.

He had been in prison then for two years. Through Else he had contact with Hans Bernd Gisevius and knew that there was much political unrest, and that the declaration of war had brought to the fore the plotters who wanted to overthrow Hitler. The nucleus of this group was in the services, the Army and the Navy. How could one join this group? Was there a better way than by volunteering to serve in the Navy?

Mrs. Niemoeller and the children did not like the idea but others on the outside, including Niemoeller's lawyers, thought it was an inspiration. On one of his wife's visits the pastor whispered to her, "What do my friends suggest with respect to my volunteering?" and she replied, "They think you had better do it." So Martin Niemoeller wrote a letter asking if he might once again command a U-boat.

The offer was the subject of widespread criticism in the United States, where it was interpreted as a patriotic desire to help Germany win the war, a "my country, right or wrong" brand of nationalism.

Looking back on the incident, Niemoeller still feels that his motivation was right for three reasons: (1) if Hitler won the war, spiritual life in Germany would be destroyed; (2) if Hitler lost the war, Germany would have little chance of a generous peace from the victors; (3) the only possible course for a German who loved his country and his church was to join the forces seeking to overthrow the Hitler regime, and thus arrange through a new government for a negotiated peace with honor. He could not fight from prison. He had to get out. And after two years he was heartsick to be free.

The maneuver did not work. Many months later he received a formal refusal signed by Admiral Keitel.

Life in prison went on. Solitary confinement with its stultifying effects went on. Contacts with others were so rare that they made a lasting impression. For instance, there was the incident that took place one day when he was lined up with others to receive blankets.

The prison camp commandant walked through. He had served as an officer in the Imperial Navy in World War I and felt a certain amount of camaraderie for Niemoeller. Seeing the prisoners lined up, he beckoned to them to gather around. When they obeyed, they observed that the commandant appeared to have been drinking rather heavily.

"Boys," the commandant said, "I am in charge here and I look after you as a father looks after his children. Is there anyone with a special wish that he would like fulfilled?"

The men looked at one another cautiously, afraid of a trap. Then a boy of eighteen stepped forward and said, "Yes, sir, I have a wish. My father has died and will be buried tomorrow. Could you give me a leave of absence to attend his funeral? I can be back in two days."

The commandant stiffened angrily. Then, arms akimbo, he shouted, "What's the matter with you? Your father has died—it is the most natural thing in the world. Your mother will die. You will die. I will die. We'll all die. There's nothing remarkable about it."

Glancing challengingly at Pastor Niemoeller, he said, "There are those who say that after death there is something. Some go to heaven and some go to hell. I shall go to hell. Isn't that so, Pastor Niemoeller?"

Pastor Niemoeller's eyes met his levelly.

"Sorry to say, sir, yes."

That was all there was to that. The boy was not allowed to go to his father's funeral. And a few weeks later the rumor went around that the commandant had been thrown from his horse. His neck was broken. He was dead. Pastor Niemoeller opened his Bible that night and read, "For judgment I did come into the world that they that see will see and they that see not may be made blind."

Martin Niemoeller was more fortunate than the eighteen-year-old boy. He was allowed to visit his dying father.

It was in early March, 1941, when he was awakened at three o'clock one morning and ordered to dress in civilian clothes.

"It has come," he thought. "Now I will be taken to be executed."

He was led outside by two SS guards and put in a car with three others. One of them said to him, "Pastor Niemoeller, we have been ordered by the Fuehrer to take you to Elberfeld. Your father is dying and wishes to see you once more and the Fuehrer has decided that his wish shall be granted."

It was a long ride to Elberfeld, 380 miles, and they did not arrive until late afternoon. They went first to police headquarters, and it was dark before Niemoeller was taken to his father's home. The entire block in which the house was located was surrounded by police.

The elder Pastor Niemoeller had had a stroke ten days before, but he was still conscious. His son was told that he could spend half an hour at his bedside but no other members of the family except his mother could be there with him. He entered quietly. His father looked at him and smiled.

"Who brought you here?" he asked.

"The Gestapo, Father."

The elder pastor turned to his wife.

"Give each man a cigar," he said, and then added with a touch of his old humor, "but not one of the good ones."

With difficulty he managed to say the few things he apparently wanted his son to know.

"Many strange and troublesome things are going on," he said, "even in our own church. You would not know this parish now. But all over the world people are praying and this gives me hope that things will not stay this way. I hope —no, I am positive—that things will change for the better."

He was very tired and remained silent awhile. Then he repeated the words Jacob spoke from his deathbed to his son, Joseph: "Behold I die, but God shall be with you, and bring you again unto the land of your fathers."

Martin Niemoeller was taken back to Sachsenhausen after this brief visit and a few days later he learned that his father had died. It was a black period for him, a period when his wife feared he might lose his mind.

Then abruptly another change was made. The Nazis had thought of a new strategic propaganda move. Word had reached them of Martin Niemoeller's interest in Roman Catholicism. What a striking blow against the Confessing Church, they reasoned, if its leader should leave the church.

In July, 1941, Martin Niemoeller was taken by car from Sachsenhausen to another prison. His companions were two Roman Catholic priests.

Their destination was Dachau.

14.

DACHAU

MARTIN NIEMOELLER once said that while he was in prison Adolf Hitler sent word to him that he could go free, provided he promised not to attack the state or criticize National Socialism's conduct of church affairs. He had been imprisoned long enough to make the offer tempting. Tempting but impossible, for that night he saw a vision, the eyes of a German youth, the youth of the future, asking him, "And why, Pastor Niemoeller, when Germany was being de-Christianized, did you do nothing about it?"

Perhaps it was this vision of the youth of the future that helped Martin Niemoeller retain his sanity while he was in prison those eight long years. Of the three places of imprisonment, the one year at Moabit, the three years at Sachsenhausen, and the last four at Dachau, the most threatening to his reason was the experience at Sachsenhausen with its long hours of nothingness.

To the average American the name "Dachau" conjures up the most dread vision of all, and by the time the American troops reached there it was a gruesome and grisly sight. That is because it was the last to be taken, and in the end it received prisoners from all the rest of the prison camps in territory that had fallen to the enemy from the west, from the north, from the east. Just before the other camps were occupied and liberated, prisoners were hastily loaded onto trains, the dead and the dying among the living. When the trains arrived at Dachau, many of the dying had died. The crematoriums could not work fast enough.

More trains came, and the corpses piled up. In the latter days of April, 1945, Martin Niemoeller remembers that the camp was one big area of corpses, corpses, corpses. There were no facilities to dispose of them so they were stacked up like firewood. This is what the occupying forces found.

But in the beginning it was not that bad.

The tourist can visit Dachau today quite easily by car or public transportation from Munich. A train runs to Dachau, which is not where the concentration camp was; a bus goes to the site at the neighboring town of Dachau Ost, East Dachau. The bus is a crowded, bouncy, commuter type of suburban bus, for Dachau Ost is no longer a camp but a town, a town in which the concrete barracks have been transformed into living quarters made bright with curtains and flower boxes and signs advertising commercial establishments. Children and dogs play in the streets. Life goes on at Dachau Ost.

But just out of town, half a mile down a country road, edged with grasses and wild flowers, is a grim sign, "Krematorium," with an arrow pointing down another road, between high concrete walls dotted with sentry boxes. At the end of the road, literally and symbolically, is the crematorium building, and around it are neat mounds, bright with the pink begonias seen in every German park and garden. Markers commemorate the "thousands of dead," the "bloody ditch" where mass executions were carried out, and the rest of Dachau's horrors.

Dachau is not a skeleton in the German closet. Signs in several languages direct the tourist to the memorial, and they come, in cars and on foot, foreigners and Germans.

Visitors may see the concrete bunkers similar to the one in which Niemoeller was kept prisoner. He was in the one next to the central building with the central kitchen, the workshops, and the showers. The space between the two buildings was a courtyard where the prisoners were exercised.

Here Martin Niemoeller was brought from Sachsenhausen, a one-day trip. He was received, surprisingly, with courtesy, was again photographed, and then taken to a bunker where he was housed with the two priests who were brought with him and a third who joined them. A table was laid and they were told they could have their meals together.

They even had an orderly. He was Old Bernhard, murderer from Hamburg, who had been sentenced to death and then given life imprisonment instead. He served as their waiter. Niemoeller had his own cell, but the door was open between his quarters and those of the priests and they were allowed to visit back and forth freely.

They became fast friends, and although the press of modern life has kept them from seeing much of one another, they have had an occasional reunion since those days. One is Johannes Neuhausler, now an assistant bishop in Munich. Another is Michael Hoeck, now regent of a priests' seminary in Freysing. The third is Nicolaus Jansen, now a prelate in Aachen. Almost eighty years of age now, Father Jansen was in his sixties then, a rugged physical specimen who swam out-of-doors even in the coldest of weather.

Himmler may have thought that these three could convert Lutheran Niemoeller, which would have been a masterful propaganda move and a blow to the Confessing Church.

The only flaw in the plan was that the three Roman Catholics were not too keen on converting Niemoeller. He did not strike them as a likely subject. Instead, what developed was a true experiment in brotherhood.

In the morning Niemoeller and the priests conducted the Roman Catholic breviary, all praying together. In the afternoon Niemoeller gave them Bible lessons, similar to the classes he had held for his confirmands. In an early burst of ambition they tried to conduct their services in Greek but soon turned to the Latin, which was more familiar to them.

In the evening before they went to bed they played cards. They had discussions, debates, friendly controversy, and the result of this mental stimulation and fellowship was that Martin Niemoeller was restored to his normal fighting spirit. He was determined to get through this thing and get through alive.

In spite of this more relaxed and easier pattern of living, Dachau was still a concentration camp. The prisoners did not know what was going to happen next, and could not close their eyes to what was happening to others around them.

Day after day they saw coffins being carried through the camp. They heard the cries of men being dragged out to be hanged, to be shot, to be taken to the crematorium, for death at Dachau was handled in a variety of hideous ways. Sometimes someone tried to escape and was shot; the others would see the bodies still hanging to the electrified fence when they were taken out for their exercise. Sometimes someone, like Lieutenant Joseph Stalin, son of the Russian dictator, in a fit of depression rushed to the electrified wire and tried to commit suicide. In the case of Stalin, the shock did not kill him, and he writhed in agony until a guard shot him and put him out of his misery.

Daily the prisoners heard the crack of shots, and each time it was a ghastly sound.

"You never get used to it," Niemoeller once said of this endless terror. "It was awful, always awful."

How much did the inmates of Dachau know of the torture and murder of the Jews brought there? Not everything, but more than they wanted to know.

"We knew that this was a great camp and that there was another part of it," Niemoeller described it on one occasion. "Through the kitchen we learned a little because the people who handed out meals for our building were the same ones who handed out meals on the other side of the camp, and one always picked up rumors. They were cautious about telling too much because you never knew who could be trusted.

"There were always a certain number of Jews in the camp and we always knew they were death candidates. Four to six of them at a time would work in the crematorium burning the others, and after a few months they were put to death and a new group came in.

"Everyone felt that there was something terrible and sinister going on in the other part of the camp, but each person had the feeling, 'If I know about it, then it exists. Leave me alone and don't tell me what you know. I don't want to know because I can't bear it.' "

Looking back on the horrors of Dachau, Martin Niemoeller draws a modern parallel to this refusal of the Dachau inmates to acknowledge the inferno in which they lived.

"It is the very same attitude," he points out, "that many people today take toward atomic warfare. They do not admit what happened at Hiroshima and what is still happening there because the knowledge is too awful to bear."

Even to his family and close friends Martin Niemoeller has never talked about the grim sights of Dachau. When he talks about Dachau, it is of the human, the lighter, the brighter, the friendly side of which he speaks. Many of his reminiscences concern a man who was very close to him there, Major Richard H. Stevens.

Major Stevens, who is now Lieutenant Colonel Richard H. Stevens, of Brighton, Sussex, England, was one of the good things that came out of Niemoeller's imprisonment. Their friendship, which began under such adverse circumstances, has continued to this day.

Stevens is an Englishman of cosmopolitan upbringing. His grandfather was a diplomat in Athens. His grandmother was

Greek. He spent his early life in Greece, attended school in Heidelberg, Germany, and became an officer in the British Army. Gifted in languages, he became a diplomat and military attaché in Iraq, Egypt, and Estonia.

In 1939, when war broke out, he was a military attaché with the British embassy in The Hague. He was one of two men who were kidnaped on the frontier on November 9, 1939; the other was Captain S. Payne Best, chief of British Secret Service in Holland. They had been tricked into believing that a group of German officers were about to revolt against Hitler and that these officers wanted to talk with them at the frontier. They kept the rendezvous, accompained by a Dutch officer, Lieutenant Dirk Klop. He was shot and killed, and they were taken as prisoners across the lines to Germany. A full account of the adventure and its aftermath is brilliantly told in Best's book, *The Venlo Incident*.

Both Best and Stevens were at Sachsenhausen but were separated and not reunited until much later. Stevens was the one with whom Pastor Niemoeller became acquainted. He first saw the Englishman while taking his exercise in the courtyard. Glancing at a cell window, he observed a man hanging onto the bars, smoking a cigarette. When he passed, the man said, "Good morning." Niemoeller replied, "Good morning, sir," in English. The second time around he took a closer look. There was something familiar about the face.

His orderly, Schwarz, had been lending him an illustrated Nazi newspaper to read. When he returned to his cell he asked Schwarz to get him the last twenty issues of the paper. Schwarz did so, and Niemoeller thumbed through them quickly until he found an issue with a story headed, "Attempt on Hitler's Life."

There were three men pictured, a German, Georg Elser on the left, and on the right, Major Stevens and Captain Best. The two men had been kidnaped so that Nazi propaganda forces would have foreign scapegoats to blame for the Buergen-braukeller plot at Munich on November 8. This had been a plot by resistance men to shoot Hitler. The Nazis, learning of it, had induced Elser, a Communist in concentration camp, to devise a machine that would blow up the conspirators while Hitler was hurried out just in time. Elser was then "captured," and the implication of the British Secret Service men was a masterful piece of propaganda to inflame the Germans against England.

Now Niemoeller knew who the familiar-looking man was. Each morning as he walked by he gave Stevens a Bible verse in English. Then abruptly, whether for this reason or not, his exercise area was changed, and he no longer passed that cell.

It was several years later that they met again. They have different recollections of how this meeting took place. Both are good stories. This is how Martin Niemoeller remembers it:

"One afternoon in 1941 I was in the courtyard at Dachau. The iron gate opened and in came the supervising officer, Beyer, with a new prisoner. I recognized Stevens and walked up boldly and said, 'Hello, Major Stevens.'

"He was taken by surprise but more surprised was Beyer. He said, 'Pastor Niemoeller, you are not allowed to know this man.' Stevens said, 'But Pastor Niemoeller and I know each other from Sachsenhausen and I shall request that we may be in the courtyard together as much as we like.'

"The commandant gave in and granted the request. He was a very nice man. They hanged him nevertheless."

Stevens' recollection is slightly different but equally interesting and significant. He writes:

"My most vivid recollection of Martin is, I think, the manner in which we first came in contact in 1940. I had been for several months in solitary confinement at Sachsenhausen when early one morning I heard the slow, measured crunch of heavy boots on the cinder path beneath the tiny window of my cell. When one is alone in a small concrete box, everything is of interest and I listened, intrigued, counting the footsteps, some forty or so in each direction.

"To look out of the window—a tiny affair about eighteen inches square just beneath the ceiling of the cell—was absolutely forbidden. But I took a chance, and as I heard the footsteps approaching, I jumped on my stool, peeped out, and tapped gently on the window. Coming toward me was a figure in the ordinary striped garb of the concentration camp. As he drew level he raised his eyes and gave me a smile of indescribable quality and with a brief gesture of the hand, half greeting, half benediction, passed beyond the range of my vision. The brief encounter had a profound effect upon me. I felt that somehow goodness, decency, and encouragement had penetrated into my solitary world of beastliness, squalor, and loneliness. Morning after morning I waited eagerly for eight o'clock and those measured footsteps, and each morning we exchanged a swift greeting that helped me through the rest of the day."

Despite his pleading, he could not get the guard to tell him who "that fellow" was.

"Be careful, Herr Fuchs," the guard warned, using Stevens' prison name. "Such information is not permitted."

After a few months the footsteps ceased.

"I listened anxiously day after day, but in vain," Stevens recalled. "I had never spoken to him, I did not know who he was, and I had seen him for but three or four seconds a day, but I had lost a trusted friend.

"Eighteen months later, in December, 1941, I was transferred to Dachau and the very first person I saw, walking with four others in the courtyard of the 'special prisoners' enclosure, was my Sachsenhausen friend. 'Who's that?' I asked a fellow prisoner urgently. He stared at me in astonishment. 'Don't you know? Why, that's Martin Niemoeller!' From the guard commander I obtained permission to join the little group. 'Gentlemen,' I said swiftly, 'I may not introduce myself, but I'm a pretty desperate and shady character in some people's estimation and if you'd rather not be seen with me, say so and I'll understand.' Martin replied for them all with the same lovely smile on his face and a twinkle in his eye, 'We're not in very great favor ourselves,' he said, 'but do join us if you wish. As for introductions, please don't worry. In any case we sometimes see the papers, you know, Herr—er—Herr Fuchs.' Thus began a deep friendship that continues undiminished to this day."

Richard Stevens played a great role in the last years of Niemoeller's imprisonment. A man of many talents, he speaks Hindu, Iraqi, Russian, German, French, is both a painter and a writer. And because of his very special position, he was allowed many special privileges. He was quartered in a large room in the bunker that had been a living room for the commanding officer. There were iron bars in front of the big window but these were the only prisonlike touch. He was allowed to paint. He was allowed to wear civilian clothes and go to Munich to shop. He was permitted to take English books from the Munich library.

Niemoeller had been reading and studying English books that Mrs. Niemoeller had obtained from friends, but it was through Richard Stevens that his study of the English language became serious. He read *A Forsyte Saga* with interest. He still remembers his thrill at obtaining three volumes of *Vanity Fair*. But the best books to him were the "Jalna" series by Mazo de la Roche. They were the substitute for the family life he so sorely missed.

With his books, his art, his excursions to the city, Stevens brought the fresh air from outside into the prison bunker. He was even permitted to have a radio set.

"How's your radio working?" Niemoeller asked him one day.

"Oh, it's no good, Martin," he said. "I can get only Munich and Berlin. I wish I could listen to London."

A few days later Stevens was beaming.

"There was a fire in my room," he reported. "The electrician had to come in. A prisoner, a nice chap. I gave him some British cigarettes. He has taken my radio along and will bring it back next week. He told the guard it was damaged by the fire."

A week later the radio was brought back. The next morning, when Niemoeller went to the shower, he came out just as Stevens was going in. They shook hands. In doing so, Niemoeller felt Stevens press something into his hand. When he got back to his cell, he opened the slip of paper and found written, in beautiful, precise handwriting the heading:

DACHAU DAILY NEWS

From then on, Stevens reported daily the news he had heard from London the night before. Feigning insomnia, he pretended to listen to music. It went on all night, lovely melodies, and underneath the news over the short-wave radio which the repairman had installed. And every morning Martin Niemoeller received the news. When Else, visiting him periodically, would try to convey some piece of information, he would smile and say, "You needn't tell me. I know it."

January 14, 1942, was Niemoeller's fiftieth birthday. As he came out of the shower Stevens, waiting to get in, shook his hand and said, "No daily news today, Martin, but Bishop of Chichester Bell and Archbishop of Canterbury Temple held a service last night for your fiftieth birthday in St. Martin's in the Fields."

"There in Trafalgar Square, next to the National Gallery," Martin Niemoeller said, "George Bell, the bishop of Chichester, had preached a sermon about me and twelve hours later I knew about it, in solitary confinement, in the concentration camp at Dachau."

15.

CHRISTMAS COMMUNION

BESIDES Niemoeller's continuing fellowship with the three Roman Catholic priests and his friendship with Richard Stevens, there were other human contacts at Dachau that made a profound impression on him. Two of them were tragic in nature.

One is the story of Old Bernhard, the orderly.

Bernhard was a sailor who had committed a murder in Hamburg and been sentenced to die when he was only nineteen years of age. This sentence was commuted to life imprisonment, and after Hitler came to power he was transferred to duty in a concentration camp. When Niemoeller and the priests came to Dachau, he was made their manservant. He was an amiable fellow, easy to talk to, humorous.

In addition to death via the crematorium many at Dachau were shot by firing squads, but some of the victims were hanged. Usually SS men did the hanging.

One day, late in the afternoon, Niemoeller walked down the long corridor to the courtyard for fresh air and passed Old Bernhard's cell. The door was open. Inside he saw Old Bernhard—a man of over seventy—sitting on his cot, weeping. Niemoeller walked in, and seeing that Old Bernhard was quite drunk, persuaded him to lie down.

On his way back some time later he looked in. Old Bernhard had sobered up a little and told his story. They had gotten

120

him to do the work of a hangman and had promised him he would receive half a bottle of brandy for every man he hanged. That afternoon he had hanged two people and drunk a bottle of brandy, and he was in agony.

He began to ask the pastor questions. He had been to Sunday school when he was a little boy, he said, before he ran away from home. He wanted to know if he was lost forever or if there was any hope for him now. Gently Pastor Niemoeller told him that Christ had died for sinners, just as he had learned it as a little boy in Sunday school.

The next morning Old Bernhard was taken to the hospital. Two weeks later he died.

In the last weeks of the war an order came from Berlin to shoot a large group of prisoners. Among those to be shot were a group of SS guards, Nazis themselves, who had fallen from favor. One of these, a boy of eighteen, had been assisting the orderly who had replaced Old Bernhard.

One night Niemoeller's cell door opened, and thinking it was one of the priests who suffered from insomnia, he scarcely looked up until he heard the sobbing of the young man.

"Pastor, I have had my trial," he burst forth. "I have been sentenced to death." Then he began to cry bitterly. "I can't die the man I am," he said. "Can I make my confession to you? I have a mother. I am an only child and she has prayed for me all my life. I can't die the man I am."

Niemoeller told him to speak out. It was a horrible story. Homosexuality was the reason for the boy's imprisonment, but his story was a recital of one sordid event after another. Pastor Niemoeller prayed for him and assured him there would be forgiveness for him as for every sinner no matter how grave the crime.

"Could I have communion?" the boy asked finally.

Pastor Niemoeller nodded. He filled his tin cup at the water tap, found a piece of bread left over from the evening meal.

The footstool was their altar. And together they took communion.

But more memorable than these two instances of his ministry was Christmas, 1944, when for the first time in concentration camp Martin Niemoeller preached a sermon. Fifteen special prisoners were told they could have a tree and sing Christmas carols. The oldest in the group, Dr. Van Dyke, a former Dutch cabinet minister, added another plea.

"I am now seventy-two years old and don't know how long I have to live," he said. "I have been in prison four years and have never heard divine services. Couldn't we Protestants have a service of our own as the Roman Catholics have every month?"

The guard hesitated. There was good reason for the inequality in the rules. A holy mass follows a set pattern and one knows what to expect, while a Protestant service entails a sermon that may contain anything. But finally he gave his consent.

Niemoeller went back to cell number thirty-two and for the first time in seven and a half years began to prepare a sermon. He was almost halfway through when he had a terrible thought.

"How can I, being a German," he thought, "preach to this congregation, a Dutchman, a British officer [Stevens], two Norwegian shipowners [Mr. Clavenus and Mr. Johanson], a Yugoslav diplomat [Dr. Popovic], and a Macedonian journalist [Tomolitsky]?

"How can I, being a German, preach the gospel to these men? Must I not, being a German, just by being a German, be an obstacle for Jesus Christ?"

The sermon was not finished and it was noon on December 24 when his cell door opened and Dr. Van Dyke came in.

"Pastor," he said, "I have something to tell you."

"Here it is," Niemoeller thought. "Now he will tell me, 'You are German and it is impossible that we listen to a German preaching the gospel because Germans tell only lies' " But he said, "Yes, go on."

I have spoken to the other five," said Dr. Van Dyke, "and we have a special request to make of you. We have not been to holy services for such a long time, we wonder if, after the service, we couldn't have holy communion together?"

Niemoeller agreed, and then he began thinking of the difficulties, of the doctrinal differences between the Lutheran and the Reformed churches in Germany which had prevented them from holding communion together because they had differing doctrines about the Holy Supper. And here he was to conduct the Lord's Supper for a Dutchman of the Reformed Church, an Englishman of the High Anglican Church, two Norwegians of Lutheran faith, a Yugoslav of the Greek Orthodox creed, and a Macedonian who felt he belonged to no particular creed.

He considered the matter, he prayed, and then he went from cell to cell and put two questions to each of the five. They were:

"Do you wish to come to Holy Supper this night to hear the voice of our Lord, Jesus Christ, directed personally to you, 'My son, thy sins are forgiven unto thee'?

"Do you wish to have a share in the body of Christ which was broken for your sins and do you wish to have a share in the blood of Christ which was poured for your sins, and will you have your share in His body and in His blood by coming to the Holy Supper and receiving this bit of bread and this sip of wine?"

The answer to both of these questions from each of the five was, "Yes, Pastor, that is what I wish."

He returned to his cell and finished his sermon. It is printed in the collection of *Dachau Sermons,* and ends with these words:

"And we, dear friends, who are cut off from the outside world, inactive spectators of all men's battles and convulsions, we who have daily many hours to gaze inwardly and to understand ourselves clearly, we who often miss so painfully the peace of mind because we do not look at God and His word but rather at mortals and their doings—should not our inward hearing be especially receptive to the tidings brought to us by the Christmas gospel? Should not the saying about the 'great joy' concern us in particular, since we know fear—fear of death as well as fear of life? Let us therefore today, on this holy Christmas Eve, beseech the Lord Jesus Christ that He, who came as a babe into a world alienated from God in order to save it, may enter also into us, bring us His salvation, and grant us His joy! Amen."

As they met in the Roman Catholic chapel, cell number thirty-four, for services and the Holy Sacrament, Martin Niemoeller saw more clearly than ever before, he believes, the will of Christ, who can bring the living church into a prison, from men of inimical nationalities and even inimical creeds, and be among them Himself. This one experience was worth eight years of imprisonment.

16.

THE FAMILY AT LEONI

M EANWHILE, life had been going on for the other members of the Niemoeller family.

Brigitte, the eldest daughter, had married. Her family did not approve of the marriage but had accepted it since life had not been too easy for any of the children under the circumstances. When Brigitte was eighteen, she had fallen in love with a doctor in military service. Her family had objected to an early engagement and sent her away to school. When she returned, just before her father's trial, she found the romance had been ended, not by her parents, but by the Nazi military.

Brigitte had planned on going to Heidelberg University. She was told, "There is no place for children of prisoners in Germany to study. You will work. Where would you like to work in war production?"

She chose the telephone company because a former U-boat comrade of her father had a position of authority there. Her first supervisor had refused to have her in his department, but then a young attorney, Nazi though he was, said, "She may work for me." That was in May, 1941. In November she and the young attorney, Benno Johannesson, were married.

"How can you marry a man who sympathizes with National Socialism?" her mother asked unhappily. Still the marriage took place, lasted through the war and the birth of three daughters, and eventually ended in divorce.

Hans Jochen, Niemoeller's eldest son, was drafted in 1940, Hermann, in 1942, both having been made to serve first in the *Arbeitsdienst,* workers' program, for six months.

Jochen adjusted fairly easily to the military life, according to Hermann, although illness prevented him from active service for a time. A prolonged case of diphtheria, followed by complications, left him paralyzed and kept him from active service until January, 1945.

Hermann, who would have been "very glad to get out of service had there been any good pretense," felt a little more resentment, but went into service, first in the Ukraine, in December, 1942, back to Sevastopol, and in September, 1943, into combat east of Crimea. On October 15, 1943, he was wounded and sent back to Silesia. A spell of malaria hospitalized him on three separate occasions and sent him to non-combat duty in Denmark. At the end of the war he was again back in Silesia and was captured by the Russians.

Jan, the third son, was the last to be drafted and he, too, was captured by the Russians at the end of the war.

Only "Mutti," Jutta, Hertha, young Tini, and Fräulein Dora remained in Dahlem. The bombings become more and more intense. One night the Dahlem Dorf farm, where prize cattle were bred, was hit, and Else Niemoeller can still remember the pitiful cries of the wounded animals.

When her husband was moved to Dachau, she began taking fortnightly trips there. It took ten hours by train to get from Berlin to Munich. She would spend the night in Munich and take the train and bus the next day to Dachau and Dachau Ost, making the last part of the journey on foot over the country roads. Since the Catholic priests were not allowed to receive visitors, her trips were happy occasions for all the clergy, as she smuggled in books, tobacco, chocolate, and even wafers for communion.

"We like to see Mrs. Niemoeller come," one of the priests wrote to a relative. "It is like a holiday."

But it was hard on her, those long hours of travel, the worry over her husband while she was away from him, the worry over the children and her household when she was away from them, the worry over her sons in service all the time. She became ill and had to stay home for three months, a very trying period for her husband, who thought she must be dying.

In the summer of 1943 a friend, Mrs. Maria Lempp, widow of a Munich publisher who had brought out some of Niemoeller's works, offered Else Niemoeller her summer house in the town of Leoni on Starnberg Lake. It was an hour by train and a half-hour by ferryboat from Munich.

The charming little house is still there, clinging to the side of a hill, eighty-three steps up from the road that skirts the lake. There is a fine view of the bright blue water, and in summertime Leoni, with its residences for wealthy Munich families and its resort hotels, has a gay, festive air. In winter it is quiet and restful.

Still ill, Else Niemoeller entered a Catholic hospital in Munich when she first arrived. The nuns treated her wonderfully and joked with her.

"Pray that the bombs don't fall," they would say. "We don't want Mrs. Niemoeller to be hurt while she's in our hospital."

The bombers hit Munich quite often, but when she was able to move out to Leoni, Else Niemoeller could breathe easily. Nightly the bombers droned overhead on their way to Munich. Invited for a vacation visit, the Niemoellers stayed on as Berlin became more and more unsafe. It was still difficult to get to Dachau, but the boats and trains continued to operate even in wartime, and though the trip took three hours, it was far easier than the ten- to fifteen-hour trip from Berlin.

When she visited Dachau, Mrs. Niemoeller never talked of

religion. The men there had enough of worship all day long. instead, she collected funny stories about the children, took more English books to read—she estimates that her husband read 400—and brought jigsaw puzzles, the harder the better.

Often the funny sayings of the children were things Jutta had said. Jutta was the gay one, always laughing and joking. She was sixteen years old in December, 1944, and family pictures of all her childhood show her impish face crinkled in a grin. And yet she could be somber and moody, too. Later on, someone remembered the day she had drawn a picture of a churchyard filled with tombstones and had put her name on one.

"Why do you do that?" a friend asked.

"Because I shall be the first to die."

Just before Christmas, 1944, Jutta went to Dachau to try to see her father, but the Gestapo, which did not allow the children to visit at this stage, refused her permission to enter. A few days after Christmas Jutta became suddenly ill with diphtheria. On the first day they could not get a doctor because they were in such a remote area across the lake. On the second day she died.

"Ha, one of your children is dead," said the guard who summoned Niemoeller to the telephone.

Niemoeller turned white.

"Would you have the grace to tell me which one?" he asked.

When the phone connection from Leoni was made, he learned it was Jutta. He took the loss stoically.

"At least we know she is in good hands now," he said.

Else Niemoeller returned to her room, shattered by grief, to find that nine-year-old Tini had put a photo of Jutta on her desk. Uuderneath it was a Bible verse that he had found and carefully copied from the Book of Job. It read, "Hitherto shalt thou come and no further." Else Niemoeller bowed before the inexorable will of God and wept.

Tini was the only one of the children to accompany her to the funeral. Hertha was ill, the other boys unable to get leave. Jutta had asked that a Christmas carol be sung at her funeral, the one that goes, "Joy, oh, joy beyond all gladness, Christ has done away with sadness." Years later, at a churchwomen's meeting in Florida, Else Niemoeller was to hear it again and re-experience its bittersweet comfort.

Two weeks later Jochen, the cheerful boy dubbed by his father "the pastor's pastor," came home on leave. Before he went back on duty he gave Hertha a sealed envelope to hold.

"Don't tell Mother," he said. "I shall not come back."

Four weeks later Mrs. Niemoeller received in the mail a Bible and personal effects labeled "relics of Hans Jochen Niemoeller." Not until another week did she get word that he had been killed in Pomerania. For the second time in three months she had to tell her husband that one of his children was dead.

She made the trip in person, and this time Martin Niemoeller went to pieces. Then she showed him Jochen's letter in which he had written, "I do not die for special idolatry. I do not die for a fatherland that has been made a god. I only die doing my duty as a German soldier. Be cheerful in hope, patient in tribulation, keep on praying."

The "pastor's pastor" had consoled his father once more.

One of the prison stories Martin Niemoeller liked to tell after his release concerned the time a high SS official came to his cell and, as Niemoeller put it, "played a soft melody."

"Oh, Pastor Niemoeller," the official said regretfully, "what a pity that such a patriot as you must be treated like this. How tragic it is. What do you think of it? How long will you stay here?"

Niemoeller hardened his heart to the soft music, the blandishments, and replied coolly, "I shall stay here no longer than Adolf Hitler lives."

This prediction turned out to be surprisingly close to the truth.

In April, 1945, Else Niemoeller made one of her periodic visits to Dachau. It looked different. Empty somehow. The typewriters were all gone from the offices.

"What is going on?" she asked her husband.

He shook his head.

"We hear they are making plans to evacuate us, in case the end comes. But I don't want to be evacuated."

He looked worried. "I don't like it."

Richard Stevens has described Niemoeller's reaction to the proposed evacuation in this way:

In April, 1945, with the sullen rumble of distant guns in our ears, excitement in the camp was intense and rumors were legion. Would the Americans, we wondered, drop paratroops on the camp? Over the "grapevine" came the news that we were to be removed to the notorious Tyrolean redoubt, there to be held as hostages and pawns of exchange. Events seemed to point to the truth of the rumor, for gradually we were joined by a number of prominent prisoners from other places—Herr Schuschnigg and his wife, Field Marshal Papagos, M. Léon Blum, and many others.

On April 26 came the order: Pack. Be prepared to move in an hour's time. Then the fun started. Martin, it must be remembered, had by that time been in captivity for eight years, one of his beloved daughters had died, and a son had been killed. His nerves were as taut as the strings of a banjo. From the "priests'" corner at the end of the row of cells came the noise of a rare rumpus. I could hear Martin's voice roaring in anger. Fragments—some of them not very canonical—of what he was saying reached my ears. . . .

"Years more as a hostage? Not me. . . . Fight . . . got a knife. . . . But I'll take one of those damn swine with me!"

One of our Roman Catholic friends came hurrying to my cell. "For goodness sake, Dick, see if you can do anything with Martin. He's in a tremendous rage, swearing that he'll kill anyone who tries to shift him. But he'll listen to you, if he'll listen to anyone."

"Ha," cried Martin, when I appeared. "Here's a man at last! You're not going to let these swine lead you away like a lamb, are you? You're not going to the Tyrol, are you, with the Americans on our doorstep?"

"I certainly am," I replied quietly.

"Then you're a damn coward!"

"Say that again and much as I love you, I'll punch you on the nose. Don't be a chump, Martin! Here, inside the camp, stiff with armed guards and surrounded by twelve feet of electrified barbed wire, we haven't a hope! We must get *outside* at all costs, then, who knows, we might start something."

To my intense relief, Martin realized that there was something in what I had said and he quieted down.

A few days later Else Niemoeller and her family heard that Dachau had been evacuated.

Hertha was staying with a friend. Her mother called her from Starnberg and told her she had heard that the prisoners from Dachau were on their way to the south by foot.

"They may be close to where you are now," she said. "Perhaps your father is with them."

"I went by bicycle," Hertha recalls, "to meet them. I knew they had to be between Munich and Starnberg and could travel only by night because the population was so aroused that the soldiers did not dare show themselves in the daytime.

"In Multheil I met them. I asked the first SS man, 'Is Pastor Niemoeller with you or not?' 'I don't know,' he said, 'let's ask someone else.' Most of the men were on the other side of a brook, camping. We walked through the whole camp, asking everyone. Finally we came to someone who told us that the so-called 'important prisoners' had been taken to Bozan by bus.

"On my way back I was stopped by an officer who said, 'Fräulein Niemoeller, I would like to speak to you for a moment.'

"I felt fear and apprehension, but I walked over to one side with him. 'Yes?' I said.

"He said, 'I have heard that the important prisoners are going to be killed after they have been used as hostages. I would like to be able to help your father. If I get to Bozan before the Americans, I'll do anything I can for him.'

"I gave the man a holy coin. Later, much later, he sent the coin back to me. Then I went back to my friends and told them. But I didn't tell my mother what the man had said. I thought it was better if she didn't know about it.

"Vati is not there," she said when she returned to Leoni. "They have put them in cars and taken them away."

17.

ESCAPE FROM DEATH

THE camp was seething with rumors those last few days of April, 1945. New arrivals were brought in to join the group of special prisoners. Among them was Kurt von Schuschnigg, former chancellor of Austria, his wife, Vera, and their daughter, Maria-Dolores, called "Sissie," who had been born in captivity. Others were M. and Mme. Léon Blum, Gabriel Piguet, bishop of Clermont-Ferrand, Field Marshal Alexander Papagos, commander in chief of the Greek forces, and several other Greek generals; General Sante Garibaldi of Italy, the German generals Franz Halder, Georg Thomas, and Alexander Baron von Falkenhausen. Also there was Captain S. Payne Best, the British intelligence officer who had been kidnaped with Richard Stevens and who had a happy reunion with his friend whom he had not seen since 1939.

This group, "a party very representative of the ravished continent of Europe," as Stevens described it in an article in the London Sunday *Express,* was congregated at Dachau, not knowing what would become of them as the war swept swiftly to its close.

Discipline among the guards crumbled. News was easily come by. The prisoners learned that Patton was about to take Frankfurt, Patch's Seventh Army might at any moment reach Munich and liberate Dachau. They hoped and prayed that they might be allowed to stay until the Americans arrived, but every day a new rumor was circulated.

Von Schuschnigg's diary in his book, *Austrian Requiem,* gives a dramatic picture of the tenseness of the last week. It reads:

April 22—We are waiting.
April 25—We are still waiting.
April 26—The Americans are closing in on Munich. We are
        . still waiting.
April 27—Evacuation. We cram into overloaded busses. Our departure was dramatic. We were told that we had to walk through the camp to the busses which stood right at the gates. We all grabbed a suitcase or a bundle containing the most necessary things. Mothers took their children by the hand and our sad little group began to walk toward the busses. When we arrived in the large square in the central camp, we halted involuntarily. A sea of emaciated figures in blue-and-white striped prison garb moved slowly in complete silence along the camp wall toward the exits. Here and there we could hear the rise and fall of hushed talk. It seemed like the last murmur of a storm, or perhaps its first warning roll. Shoulder to shoulder, thirty-five thousand shadows of human beings moved on. They were to march southward—away from the front. There was no transportation for them.

A narrow aisle was being kept open by the guards through which we were to go. Suddenly, as we passed, a worn-out hand stretched from the mass! Here someone you knew, there a familiar face smiled tiredly. At first only a few, then more and more, hundreds, thousands—hands were raised in salute—some of them in the Hitler salute by force of habit—others with the closed fist. They were friends—human beings—men and women—Austrians.

It was perhaps the most impressive moment of all those years.

In a later entry Von Schuschnigg wrote, "Finally I got the particular joy of shaking the hand of Pastor Niemoeller who had done so much—not only for his fellow prisoners but for all Germans—by his courage and upright attitude; more than they realize today. We had admired him for many years."

The convoy moved through Munich. Best, in his book, *The Venlo Incident,* described it as "lurching like a ship at sea as we bumped our way over rubble and hastily filled bomb craters—the ruins were still smouldering and the air was thick with smoke." He had known prewar Munich but he scarcely recognized this endless stretch of gutted buildings.

About midnight they bogged down in the ruins of Rosenheim, a small town but an important railway junction that had been pulverized by air attacks. One of the busses plunged nose first into a bomb crater near the remnants of the railway station. As they worked to get it out, sirens wailed and the droning throb of aircraft could be heard coming nearer and nearer. It was a bright moonlight night and the effect was anything but pleasant. Fortunately the aircraft were bound for a target some miles away and soon the bombs could be seen bursting in the distance.

At dawn they arrived at Camp Reichenau near Innsbruck. It was a filthy place, bedbug-ridden, unsanitary, uncomfortable, but spirits were high among the prisoners. Perhaps the Americans would intercept them.

At dark came the order, *"Kolonne startbereit um acht Uhr"* —"The column will be ready to move at eight o'clock." They traveled slowly, uncomfortably, through the night. For hours they were halted in the narrow Brenner Pass while German military columns fleeing from the Italian front roared past. In daylight, a tempting target for the numerous low-flying aircraft, they emerged on the Italian side of the Brenner and turned east up the Puster Valley. An Allied plane spotted them and swooped down.

"But as in the Greek tragedies of old," Stevens wrote, "the gods sent a scarf of mountain mist to envelop us at the critical moment, and the aircraft roared over and away, in search of other targets."

A few hours later they reached a village, known by the German name of Niederdorf or the Italian name, Villa Basta, near the Lago de Braies or Pragser Wildsee. The convoy halted and while they stretched their cramped legs, an SS officer sought to make arrangements for them to stay.

Everything was in a state of confusion and the prisoners were uneasy at the way things were going. They were supposed to be under the command of an Untersturmfuehrer named Stiller but they were also being guarded by SS and SD detachments commanded by a Lieutenant Bader who aroused their suspicions by his manner. As they waited to see what disposition was to be made of them and by whom, a constant stream of German military trucks, laden with soldiers and civilians, furniture, equipment, and even livestock, screamed past. Groups of Italian patriots wearing red neckbands waved friendly greetings, especially when they recognized General Garibaldi.

Finally their guards marched them to the town hall where they arranged beds out of straw on the floor. When they had been left to themselves, a council of war was held. Everyone was edgy about the presence of the SS. It was entirely possible that they would be liquidated before help could come. Obviously the German Army was not far off. The German generals assured them they would be in friendly hands if the German Army could reach them.

Captain Best in *The Venlo Incident* makes quite a point of this bitter animosity of the German professional generals toward the Nazis.

"They were all men who had hated Hitler bitterly," he wrote, "hated him most of all because he had involved their country in a war which from the first they had declared could not be won."

He noted that they seemed to derive a "certain satisfaction from German defeat since it tended to prove that war waged in defiance of established General Staff theory could never be successful." They were soldiers who regarded war dispassionately, as though it were a game of chess—"as long as they were players they devoted their best skill to the game, planning their moves and moving their pieces without thought of any purpose beyond that of playing strictly to rule. Hitler was for them an intrusive amateur who, ignorant of the rules, did not play the game."

Two of the generals, Thomas and Von Bonin, volunteered to walk to the village and telephone German headquarters in an effort to reach General Vietinghof, who was in command of the German southern armies and was a friend of Von Bonin. In their full uniforms and with nothing to show they were under arrest, the generals set off down the road.

Some of the others, Niemoeller, Stevens, and Best among them, procured some bottles of wine from the cellar of the Hotel Bachmann nearby. They saw to it that their guard got more than his share of the wine. When they were all in a friendly mood, Best suggested that they drink *"Bruederschaft,"* assuring the guard that they were his friends and would stand by him.

"Yes, I know you are my friend and would help me if you were alive," said the guard, "but here is the order for your execution; you won't be alive tomorrow."

"What nonsense is that?" Best said. "Surely no one is going to be such a fool as to shoot any of us at this stage of the war. Why, the whole lot of you will be prisoners yourselves in a day or two."

"No, it is quite certain. See, here it is in black and white— an order from the Reichssicherheitsdienst in Berlin."

And Best and the others read: "The following prisoners must not be allowed to fall into the hands of the enemy but must be liquidated," and there were listed the names of Von Schuschnigg, Blum, Niemoeller, Schacht, Mueller, Falkenhauser, Thomas, Halder, Stevens, and Best.

The plan, the guard told them, was to shoot them at the hotel with tommy guns, and then set the hotel on fire. He didn't like the idea. With tommy guns, half the people would not be properly dead; the bullets were too small and you couldn't aim properly. A lot of them would still be alive when the place was set on fire.

"Herr Best, you are my friend," he said with drunken devotion. "I will tell you what we will do. I will give you a sign before they start shooting and you come and stand near me so that I can give you a shot in the back of the head—that is the best way to die—you won't know anything about it. I am a dead shot, never miss."

With this reassuring thought they went to bed. Niemoeller slept soundly that night—"either due to lack of nerves or to no lack of red wine," he later recalled cheerfully, but several of the others waited up for Thomas and Von Bonin to report back. At 3 A.M. they returned with news that Vietinghof promised to send an officer with a company of infantry.

The officer arrived later that morning with his men but he was a mild-mannered young man, hesitant about taking over authority from the SS.

Best describes the war of nerves which then took place with the several leaders cornering their commander, Stiller. He had better not start anything, they said. Many of the men were on their side and had turned over their arms to the prisoners. If any shots were fired, there would be wholesale slaughter. Stiller assured them of his good will but said he could not speak for Lieutenant Bader and the SS. In that case, they said, Stiller must turn over his command to Captain Best. He was to tell Bader of their military support and call a meeting at twelve noon. Stiller agreed.

The council of war adjourned, feeling relieved at the results, only to run into more trouble. As they went outside they met some of the other prisoners who told them a new plan had been formulated without their knowledge. General Garibaldi had contacted some of the patriots and they were to attack at midnight and try to overpower the German guards.

The committee was in a dilemma. A conference was called. Garibaldi was amenable to any change that would be in the general interests of all. He agreed to hold his men in reserve and try the German Army first.

At noon in an atmosphere of suspense a meeting of all the prisoners was called. Stiller announced that henceforth they would take their orders from Captain Best. The young German officer, after conversation with Von Bonin, who agreed as his superior to accept all responsibility, had his men train their machine guns on the SS trucks. Von Bonin and Best walked over to Bader and his men and said, "Throw down your arms or those guns will go off." They threw them down and the Italian patriots quickly whipped them up. Bader became surprisingly humble and asked if they might have some gas so they could move on.

They were not yet liberated but they were free, and a mood of relief and relaxation came over the prisoners. Someone had investigated a peculiar seating arrangement in the trucks in which the Gestapo had been traveling and had come across 150 British Red Cross food parcels which they had stolen. The women in the party did the cooking. They dined sumptuously—no small trick for a party of 136 men, women, and children, ranging in age from four to seventy-three, and of seventeen different nationalities. They moved into a hotel farther up in the mountains, the Hotel Prags Wildbad, a big resort hotel, and undertook to make themselves comfortable until they were taken over by the Americans.

Three days later a plane, audible but hidden in mists, dropped leaflets announcing the unconditional surrender of all German armed forces in Italy.

And early on the morning of May 5 Captain John Atwell of the American Fifth Army led his company to the hotel and took formal charge of the prisoners.

Nothing could have exceeded the kindness, the forethought, and generosity of our American rescuers [Stevens later wrote in tribute to them]. With their advent, a veritable cascade of food, clothing, smokes, and drinks descended upon us. No effort which contributed in any way to our comfort or happiness was any trouble at all; even individual wishes were quietly, courteously, and sympathetically received—and met with disconcerting swiftness.

The occasion was not without its moments of comic relief. One of the first acts of the Americans was characteristic of our cleanliness-conscious country. Everyone was miserably dirty. Through an ingenious system Atwell's men arranged a device which brought up icy water from the lake, passed it through the radiators of half-a-dozen trucks, and emerged in the showers of a tented enclosure piping hot. The former prisoners lined up for baths—politely letting ladies be first.

In the first party was General von Falkenhausen, a most charming old gentleman [Stevens wrote of the occasion]. Before the war he had been military adviser to General Chiang Kai-shek, but Hitler, with threats of reprisals against his family, had compelled him to return to Germany shortly after the war started. His crime had been that, as military governor of Belgium, he had treated the Belgians "too humanely." When he left China, he had been given as a mark of esteem a superb robe of honor, a heavy silk affair richly embroidered with silver and gold. In this he went off to his bath.

He was a great favorite with the ladies and his emergence

from the bathing establishment was greeted with much applause. Gaily the old gentleman joined the ladies on the veranda, turning this way and that and proudly exhibiting his gorgeous robe. Alas! What he did not know was that at back it was split from collar to hem! The general retired in greater haste and confusion than he had ever done in the course of his long and distinguished career!

The next morning the American divisional commander arrived with news that his transport was urgently required elsewhere and he would be grateful if they would prepare to move, though it was not compulsory, and anyone who felt unequal to the trip could wait and rest. Some of the prisoners were nervous about the American speed and efficiency.

"What I'm frightened of," said one of them, "is that the Americans will say, 'Who's this guy? A Ruritarian? O.K., stick a two-cent stamp to the seat of his pants and post him to Ruritania.' "

The American general allayed these fears. "I cannot," he said, "guarantee to send everyone where he wants to go, but I can and do promise that no one shall be sent where he doesn't want to go."

They were taken to Verona, a long, interesting, but arduous drive over broken and flooded roads. They were due to arrive at seven in the evening but arrived at one in the morning.

At eight in the morning they boarded a plane for Naples. It was the first step of the long voyage home. At the airport the pastor was met by a young Jewish lieutenant in the American Army.

"I was one of your confirmands at Dahlem," he said.

For Martin Niemoeller, liberation was more difficult than imprisonment at first, because of several things. First of all was the natural letdown, the state of shock that set in after the tense and terrible ordeal they had all been through. Second was his worry over his family. He feared for his wife's health and sanity under the strain. He had no idea where Brigitte was except that she and her child were somewhere in Germany. He had received word that Hermann was wounded and listed as "missing" in Russia. Jan also was "missing" in Russia. Hertha and Tini were with their mother, but how were they?

His American captors kindly established Niemoeller in the Parco Hotel for a rest, but for some unexplained reason they did not fulfill his request to notify his wife that he was safe. On May 15 Bishop G. Bromley Oxnam visited him, and he poured out his frustrations and annoyance.

"Such a simple thing, just a telegram would do it," Niemoeller said. "My wife is twenty-eight kilometers out of Munich. Her residence is well known. Why should they refuse this?"

Chaplain A. Stanley Trickett, who was present at the interview with Bishop Oxnam, telephoned headquarters at once and according to the bishop "learned that the request was lying upon some desk awaiting formal action." The bishop telephoned General Spofford and explained the pastor's concern. Within two hours a telegram from General Alexander was sent and the next day word reached the pastor.

Bishop Oxnam interviewed Niemoeller about his experiences and views for a story later published by *The Christian Century*. He reported that after the pastor's fears were allayed that he autographed the bishop's New Testament, signed "shortsnorter" bills for the chaplains, and wrote a few lines in a notebook for Chaplain Philip H. Oxnam, the bishop's son.

"We left him in a happier mood, a strong man made stronger by suffering, a warrior who had moved from the war of nations to the battle of the spirit, a symbol of Christian resistance to pagan tyranny, a man who may yet become a power in Germany."

Two days later Dorothy Thompson interviewed Pastor Niemoeller. Excerpts from her report on the meeting include:

If a man spends eight years in prison, four behind barbed wire, and then is placed in solitary confinement for refusing to render unto Caesar the things that are God's, and if meanwhile his sons are killed or missing in action or are forced to fight for their father's jailers, several things can happen to him. He can find that God has forsaken him, he can become cynical, he can take refuge in other wordly mysticism against the realities of life, or he can become strengthened and purified to an incandescent faith and an unassailable inner freedom.

To Martin Niemoeller the last has happened. All the trials of Job have befallen him and his family. Of his seven children, only two are certainly alive and with their mother. He has seen the country which he was too sternly honest to reject as his own defeated, abased, ruined, and despised as he foresaw it would be when it bent its knee to the golden calf of evil power.

He does not know whether in one hundred years Germany will again take its place in civilization with honor but he knows wherein he believes. . . .

He is a man from whom fear forever has flown. He is boyishly slim, wiry, nervous, but disciplined. In full simplicity and humility his brown eyes look steadily as he speaks and his smile is alight with kindness and peace.

It was Dorothy Thompson who first brought the heart-warming and comforting description of Pastor Niemoeller to his family at Leoni, although they had heard of his liberation. Had he but known, he would have been spared much anguish at Naples, for they had heard the news even before the American Army had arrived at Villa Basta, when the German Army had taken over.

"It was on May 2 that friends came rushing to the house." Mutti Niemoeller has told the story many times. "They cried, 'Have you heard the news? Your husband has been liberated.' "

She turned on the radio. Pastor Niemoeller, Von Schuschnigg, and Léon Blum had been liberated, came the announcement. She listened to the same news broadcast six times—the same thing over and over. It didn't say how, it didn't say where, but she didn't care. For the moment it was enough. He had not been killed. And the war was over.

18.

THE UNFORTUNATE PRESS CONFERENCE

The press release that appeared in American newspapers said that Kurt von Schuschnigg, the former chancellor of Austria, had been invited to attend the press conference in Naples on June 5, but had "decided not to" do so. How often friends of Martin Niemoeller, finding hindsight easier than foresight, have wished that he, too, had declined to attend that unfortunate conference.

It was Niemoeller's debut, his first postwar presentation to the American public, and it created the most disastrous impression possible. Much of the misunderstanding about Niemoeller, many of the unfortunate and untrue rumors can be traced back to that bungled press conference. It was not because of what he said but because of the way he said it. Praeses Koch might have sighed with good reason, "Oh, Martin, did you have to say it just that way?"

David L. Ostergren, a major and chief of the chaplains' section of the Peninsular Base Section, Southern District, felt so strongly that the interview had been misunderstood that he later wrote an interpretive letter to the American people. He told how Niemoeller had impressed him in the month they had spent together in Naples as a kind man with a remarkable sense of humor and a genuinely humble nature.

"When we in Naples tried to make a hero of him, he denied

that he had suffered greatly and said that there were many who had suffered more than he," wrote Ostergren.

Niemoeller and Ostergren dined together on the day set for the first big interview with thirty-two correspondents at the Parco Hotel on Capri. Niemoeller was nervous and afraid that his English would be inadequate. He could speak and read the language but sometimes had difficulty understanding it.

Ostergren did not attend the interview but saw Niemoeller that evening and asked him the results. He did not criticize the press but said he was bewildered by all the questions put to him. He was also disappointed that he had been unable to explain his thoughts in his own way.

Ostergren then spoke to one of the American officers who was present at the interview.

"It was a shame the way the reporters heckled Pastor Niemoeller," said the officer. "They shot questions at the man right and left and finally got him all mixed up. It was the most unfair interview any man could be given."

The interview was emblazoned in American papers the next day and these were some of the messages they conveyed:

PASTOR NIEMOELLER BELIEVES GERMANS UNFIT FOR DEMOCRACY

HITLER'S PRISONER SAYS, "IN WAR GERMAN DOES NOT ASK RIGHT OR WRONG: HE WANTS TO FIGHT AND DIE WITH GERMANS"

HOPES TO VISIT ENGLAND AND U.S. TO APPEAL FOR RELIEF FOR "GOOD" PEOPLE IN REICH . . . THEY FEEL NO RESPONSIBILITY

How were these answers brought out? One of the first questions asked the pastor was, "Why did you oppose National

Socialism?" His answer was, "For religious reasons." The reporters did not follow this up with, "What do you mean by religious reasons?" They assumed that Niemoeller was referring to Hitler's desire to take over the management of church affairs. Thus the idea was conveyed to America that Niemoeller had opposed Hitler only because the church was persecuted, that until his own interests were threatened, he had no complaint against Hitler.

Ostergren, in his own conversations with the pastor, had followed up the phrase "for religious reasons" by asking, "What do you mean by religious reasons?" To which Niemoeller had replied:

"Some people opposed National Socialism for political reasons, some for economic reasons, and some for religious reasons. My reasons for opposing National Socialism were religious. They include all the above reasons and go deeper than any of them. For example, National Socialism encouraged socialization of marriage, wherein a Nazi was encouraged to have children not only with his wife but with other women as well in order to build up the man power of Germany. This violated the commandment 'Thou shalt not commit adultery.' National Socialism took over property in a way that could be called nothing else than stealing. This violated the commandant 'Thou shalt not steal.' Without cause National Socialism cruelly murdered Jews and many others. This violated the commandant 'Thou shalt not kill.'

"National Socialism disregarded the sacredness of the individual. The individual had no importance of his own. He was important only in so far as he made a contribution to the state. This violated one of the central doctrines of Christianity, namely the sacredness of human personality. Thus you can see what I meant by 'religious reasons.' "

Obviously the answer to the question, "Why did you oppose National Socialism?" should have been, "Because they advocated violation of moral laws and civil laws, disregarded individual rights, and persecuted the Jews."

Instead, by using the phrase "religious reasons," Niemoeller laid the groundwork for the charge that he was "a Nazi at heart." The reporters did not understand that his careful phrasing was in keeping with his Lutheran upbringing. *Time* magazine in trying to explain this situation, in March, 1947, said, "Few have understood that for a traditional Lutheran religious grounds are the only valid ones for opposition to the state." It further quoted Luther in his directive that civil authority, no matter how evil or foolish, must be opposed only when it encroaches on the spiritual realm and orders its subjects to go against God's commandments.

"You must know that from the beginning of the world," wrote Luther, "there was rarely a prince who was wise and even more rarely one who was pious. They are usually the biggest fools and the worst criminals on earth." Consequently, he advised, "Be unto them humble subjects as long as they do not overreach themselves and wish to be shepherds instead of executioners."

Equally misunderstood was the statement that the pastor made concerning the atrocities in concentration camps. He said that he himself had been "shocked and shattered" by the pictures, but that he thought the great masses of German people were unaware that such crimes had been committed.

"But you are mistaken," he added, and this appeared in bold-face type in the newspapers, "if you think any honest person in Germany will feel personally responsible for things like Dachau, Belsen, and Buchenwald. He will feel only that he was misled into believing in a regime that was led by criminals and murderers."

Asked about his own treatment in concentration camp, Niemoeller again erred on the side of truth. He said that he had been treated with "gentlemanliness" because he was a "personal prisoner of Adolf Hitler."

He did not go into details as to the "gentlemanliness" of Adolf Hitler which had put him in solitary confinement, fed him on bread and water for two years, almost caused him to lose his health, his sight, his sanity, then made him a daily witness to murder, human destruction, and disintegration for five more years. In his humble way he meant that he had not suffered as much as others—he had not been beaten or put to death.

He also told reporters that he hoped to visit America and try to explain the "German mentality" to the Anglo-American world. On the chances for democracy in Germany, he tried to express his honest convictions:

"It may be that Germany can become democratic, but you have got to face the fact that the German people are not adapted to the sort of democracy that exists in Britain and the United States.

"The German people are different from the British and American peoples. They like to be governed; they like to feel authority. You cannot imagine how the German people were looking for authority when old Hindenburg died. You cannot imagine the hypnotic effect of a man like Hitler on the inner recesses of the German soul."

Leigh White, one of the correspondents who attended the press conference, described many of the reporters as "hostile." It must be remembered that most of them were war correspondents, hardly conditioned by their experiences to think kindly of any German. The belief already was common that no German was to be trusted, none would own up to having been a Nazi, and all were suspect.

Their questions seemed more and more like rapid machine-gun fire, and Niemoeller became increasingly nervous and agitated. Finally one of the correspondents asked him about his offer to fight for his country. Niemoeller tried to explain why he had made the offer. Then another asked if it were true that his son, Jochen, had been killed in action. Niemoeller said it was.

The reporter stood, leveled his finger at Niemoeller, and shouted:

"Then you admit your son died for Adolf Hitler."

And with that Niemoeller went completely to pieces.

Why had the reporters been so antagonistic? Because they did not know about the German church struggle and the many outspoken opponents of Hitler who had been jailed? Because they knew Germans only as the collective enemy? Because, as one cynical German has suggested, "It was the official American line to refuse to acknowledge that there had been any German resistance"?

Why had Niemoeller, instead of quoting the Bible verses that had comforted him most in prison, chose to plunge into politics? Because he is Martin Niemoeller and must speak the way he must, as he did in the pulpit in Dahlem.

But the damage was done. Here is a typical letter that appeared in a newspaper column following the interview:

Before we begin to wave the flags and hail Pastor Niemoeller as a martyr, we would do well to read over not once but a dozen times your very enlightening article on him. His Nazi views expressed are audacious and shocking. The pastor admits he did not suffer much during his imprisonment, as he was "treated with gentlemanliness as Hitler's personal prisoner." He used his time to perfect his English in order to tour the world explaining the German mentality. He did not oppose nazism politically and offered his services as U-boat commander because to him it was "morally indefensible not to serve when he had three sons serving with the Wehrmacht. Moreover, in war a German does not ask if it is right or wrong." ... And while we here are still reeling from the shock of the atrocity camps, we are given the final dose, "You are mistaken if you think any honest German will feel personally responsible for Dachau, Belsen, or Buchenwald."

All the answers that had been misunderstood, all the points that lacked clarification are used here to give a picture of Martin Niemoeller, a completely distorted picture.

Bishop Oxnam spoke to a Hollywood film producer shortly after the unfortunate Naples incident. The producer had been interested in doing a movie on Niemoeller's life but now had given up the idea.

"He is done," said the producer. "What he needed was a good public-relations man."

19.

HOMECOMING AT LAST

LIKE other families, the Niemoellers dreamed of the happy homecoming of the man of the house, but for five long weeks there were frustrations and unexplained delays.

There were two bright spots in the period of waiting. The first was the visit of Dorothy Thompson to the house at Leoni and the first eyewitness account that Mrs. Niemoeller had of her husband—how he looked, how he acted, how his health appeared to be. Then on May 15 neighbors told her that Jan had spoken on the radio. He was well and he would be home soon. Later she learned that a nephew of Molotov in Dachau had promised Niemoeller that upon his release he would find Jan. Actually Jan was not liberated until 1948.

Mutti, Hertha, Tini, and Fräulein Dora waited in the lakeside cottage. But Pastor Niemoeller was not brought there. Instead, he was taken from his rest cure in Naples and flown first to France, where the prisoners were housed in a wretched camp, then to Frankfurt, where he was greeted by the mayor as a national hero.

The confusion was intensified when he was taken from this enthusiastic welcome to an interrogation camp in Wiesbaden and put behind barbed wire. American reporters came to talk to him there, and he was the Niemoeller they loved to quote, caustic, undiplomatic, good copy.

"The Americans say I have been liberated," he snapped

at them. "If I have been liberated, please tell me why I am behind barbed wire?"

He went on a hunger strike. Four days later he was released. He and his old friend, Pastor Hans Asmussen, got a car and started out for Munich, making their way over detours and through barricades. In the middle of the night they were stopped by a group of American soldiers and asked to show their passport.

"Don't tell me you are Martin Niemoeller?" one of the soldiers cried out.

"Do you know what you are in America? A national hero," the soldier assured him. "Boys, come here and meet a hero. Let me kiss you."

"And," Martin Niemoeller chuckled as he told the story later, "he kissed me."

At five thirty in the morning of June 24 Else Niemoeller heard a voice under the window in the house on the hill overlooking Starnberg Lake. She roused herself, looked out.

Down below stood a gaunt, haggard man. He smiled at her. The eyes were tired, there were lines in the face, but the luminous smile was the same. She hurried down to the door to let him in. Then she took him to the bedside of the sleeping Tini. She shook the boy by the shoulders. He opened his eyes.

"Do you know who this is?" his mother asked.

Tini blinked. Then he smiled.

"It is Vati," he said.

After his experiences of the past few weeks, from verbal brickbats to roadside kisses, Niemoeller was understandably bewildered. It was a relief, therefore, to meet an American who was an unqualified partisan on the day he returned to Leoni.

This man was Willard Simpkins, a New York stockbroker, who had long been an admirer of Niemoeller. Even before the United States entered the war, his interest had been kindled by the accounts of the pastor's bravery in the face of nazism. In March, 1945, when Simpkins went to Europe with the United States Strategic Bombing Survey, a civilian investigating board to study the results of air damage to Germany, he hoped to meet Martin Niemoeller.

Simpkins and other members of the Survey were living at the end of the war in one of Mad Ludwig's famous castles near Leoni on the Starnberg Sea. When he learned that Mrs. Niemoeller was nearby, he went to see her, knowing that the pastor was in Frankfurt. By this time Mrs. Niemoeller also knew her husband was in Frankfurt. She told Simpkins she wanted to go to her husband immediately.

"You stay here," Simpkins advised her. "I know American methods. The weekend is coming up. He'll arrive here in Leoni on Saturday."

Niemoeller did arrive on Saturday, and that afternoon he and his family called on Simpkins at the castle and received a hospitable welcome. They were entertained at dinner, then taken for a motorboat ride on the Starnberger See. Martin Niemoeller had the pleasure of seeing his son, Tini, steer a boat at the same age, eleven, that he himself had first done so. Young Tini was deluged with chocolates and cigarettes which he gave to his father.

The pastor had to return to Frankfurt for futher interrogation, and the Survey flew him back in their DC-3. Simpkins was shocked at the treatment given Niemoeller at army headquarters in Frankfurt. The Niemoellers were kept standing for two hours until Niemoeller, swallowing his pride, asked for a chair for Mrs. Niemoeller, but stiffly refused one for himself. He was treated with suspicion, and when a young lieutenant said to the colonel, "This is Martin Niemoeller," the colonel corrected him with a stern, "You mean here is a man who purports to be Martin Niemoeller."

"You're missing a great opportunity for propaganda with the German youth," Simpkins told an army official.

"It's been destroyed now," the official said.

"Yes," Simpkins agreed, "but you helped destroy it."

While the Niemoellers were in Frankfurt, their eldest daughter Brigitte arrived in Leoni. She had been in Berlin but had been evacuated to Kuxhaven on the North Sea with her husband and some of his family. When she learned that her father was alive, she insisted on going to him. She was expecting a second baby momentarily and her husband neither understood nor sympathized with her desire to travel. But through a secretary who had known her father she obtained permission from the English military commander and left in one of the first cars permitted to travel.

She arrived in Leoni on July 20 and Fräulein Dora was amazed and aghast at seeing her. But Pastor Niemoeller merely smiled as if he had been expecting her and said, "Ah, you are here."

Brigitte, who had not seen him for four years, thought he looked well and felt as though she had never been away from him. Many others besides his family have commented on this characteristic of Martin Niemoeller of picking up the threads as if they had never been broken, of never seeming a stranger to anyone who has ever known him.

Martin Niemoeller's immediate inclination was to get back to work as vigorously as if he had never stopped. His family and friends begged him to take a vacation, to rest, but instead he plunged into writing letters, talking with churchmen, attempting to think out how the church should move forward.

On August 27, 1945, the first postwar meeting of the German Protestant Church was held at Treysa. Stewart Herman, American clergyman and writer, has described this conference in his book, *The Rebirth of the German Church,* as an occasion full of emotional tension from the first day to the last. The setting chosen by Bishop Theophilus Wurm was a small Hessian town where traditional costumes are still seen and "women wear their hair in tight little topknots like apples on their heads." But the setting was the only touch of serenity.

The old antagonists were present. Bishop Meiser and Bishop Marahrens represented the conservative Lutherans, and Martin Niemoeller the liberals, the reformers, calling for a complete housecleaning, insisting that they face facts and admit that something had gone wrong with their religious life, or this cancer of nazism could not have taken hold.

Niemoeller in his talks referred to the *Schuldfrage,* the guilt question, of which much more was to be heard. Herman commented that many pastors looked as if they would have been more comfortable discussing the *Schulfrage,* the school question.

"Repentance requires conversion, not restoration," was the theme of his message. The people of their country could not be urged to repent until their spiritual leaders had done so, he said. But it was not a popular theme.

You should have seen that self-satisfied church at Treysa [he was later to write to a friend]. "We led the people correctly. The church has not failed. We preached the pure doctrine and did not walk the wrong ways of the German Christians." ... And then they talk of the only pure doctrine of Lutheranism and of the necessity of divorcing ourselves from the Calvinists and similar blasphemies, when all the time God's knife is right at their throats but they don't want to be told the truth.

The Confessing Church and its fraternal council tried to have adopted a "Word to Pastors," which stressed the necessity for repentance and conversion, but it failed in its original form and strength, indicating that the sympathies of the majority were not united on this issue.

Instead, they busied themselves with organization. Three

forms of reorganization were considered and abandoned: reorganization under the Nazi constitution of 1933, reorganization under the old outdated constitution of 1922, and reorganization under the emergency government of the Confessing Church. Finally it was decided that instead of any of these forms, all existing bodies would be merged into a new group to be called the Evangelical Church in Germany, abbreviated to be called by its German initials, the EKID.

A Council of Twelve was elected as a provisional church government. Bishop Wurm was made chairman and Pastor Niemoeller vice-chairman until the regularly elected synod could meet.

It was a compromise, but many observers felt that getting Martin Niemoeller and Bishop Marahrens together under one roof was an indication of church unity. Karl Barth who attended as a delgate of the Confessing Church said that "worse compromises had been made." Bishop Neiser hailed it as a hopeful trend. And the aged Rev. Pastor von Bodelschwingh, who was to die six months later, said, "God grant us one step forward."

For Martin Niemoeller it had been a tremendous strain coming only a few months after his release from prison. On the final day of the conference he became unconscious. His condition was diagnosed as a heart attack and he was sent back to Leoni to rest. But he was hardly in a restful frame of mind.

20.

STUTTGART STATEMENT

In October an old friend came to Leoni, the
Rev. Ewart Edmund Turner of Syracuse, New York, whom
they'd known in the early days in Dahlem. The Rev. Mr.
Turner now was a war correspondent for a religious news
service, in cooperation with the American Committee for the
World Council of Churches. This group was interested in
getting in touch with German pastors and German churches.
At the same time, the Department of Defense wished to reach
the German people through some organized group.

Ironically, the church was the only organized body that
had survived the war. The school system was destroyed.
Radio, press, unions, political parties were not functioning.
Only the church, which Adolf Hitler had tried to destroy
within six months of taking power in Germany, remained
intact. Thus the first reporter to reach Germany from the
United States was the religious service's Rev. Mr. Turner.

There were only four press centers in Germany at the time:
Berlin, Wiesbaden, Nuremberg, and Munich. Turner set up
an improvised press camp near Leoni. Down the road was an
Air Force officers' rest camp in a former hotel. Here he could
secure food. There was a motor pool across the road to furnish
transportation. Nearby on the lake was a communications
unit set up in a castle. He thus had the three basic necessities,
and while it was primitive—you could scarcely hear over the

telephone in those days—it was usable. And best of all, he was near his friends, the Niemoellers.

Turner quickly observed that his old friend was depressed and discouraged. There had been a letdown after the enthusiasm at Treysa. The Lutheran Church of Bavaria, never in sympathy with him, had not invited him to speak from their pulpits. He had freedom but no work. In his bedroom he sat at his typewriter, writing as many as thirty-five letters a day, for want of something else to do.

But worst of all, he felt he had no message, nothing to preach if he had had a place to preach. Daily he and Turner took long walks, and Niemoeller talked out his unhappiness. He and Turner discussed the fact that the Christian Church had to face up to an acknowledgment of its responsibilities. This would be the church's contribution to the new beginning of reconciliation.

But in spite of these daily pep talks, Niemoeller continued to be unhappy and nervous. To get him out of his black mood Turner suggested they take a trip to Berlin. On the way they would stop off in Stuttgart where the newly formed Council of the Evangelical Church of Germany was to hold a meeting with visiting foreign church dignitaries. This event in itself was highly significant considering that it was taking place less than six months after the cessation of hostilities. Among the visitors brought together by the Provisional Committee of the World Council of Churches were Dr. W. A. Visser't Hooft, general secretary of the committee, Pastor Alphons Koechlin of Basel, Professor Hendrik Kraemer, of Holland, Pastor Pierre Maury of Paris, the Right Rev. George K. A. Bell, bishop of Chichester, and the Rev. Gordon Rupp of England, the Rev. S. C. Michelfelder, of the Lutheran World Federation, the Rev. Dr. Samuel McCrea Cavert, general secretary of the Federal Council of Churches, and Stewart W. Herman, all of the United States.

A friendly officer was in charge of the military government at Leoni. He put an American star on the Niemoeller car so they could cross lines to Berlin. In mid-October they set out. On the way to Stuttgart they stopped to visit a pastor friend of the Niemoellers.

"Did you know you are to preach in Stuttgart?" asked the pastor's wife. "I just read about it in the paper."

"I have nothing to preach about," Niemoeller said glumly.

Neither Turner nor Mrs. Niemoeller knew whether he would fall in with the plans to have him preach. They had no idea whether or not there was a positive word in him.

When they arrived at the cathedral, a man came up to them.

"Did you know your sermon is to be broadcast?" he asked.

For the first time Niemoeller showed a return of his dry wit.

"Well," he commented, "if I can get through the sermon I will get through the broadcast as well."

He turned to his wife.

"Give me a Bible."

She did.

"Give me a text."

She opened the Bible to Jeremiah 14.

According to Dr. Visser't Hooft, Pastor Niemoeller compared the words of Jeremiah with the lament which was now the daily bread of Christians in Germany. Wrote Dr. Visser't Hooft:

Even in the church it was not yet sufficiently understood that the last twelve years had been a visitation from God. It was not enough to blame the Nazis. The church also had to confess its guilt. Would the Nazis have been able to do what they had done if church members had been wholly faithful? A Gestapo man had asked him—and it had been a great joy to him to hear it—"Why have the churches in all these years of war not prayed for victory?" But the church had not spoken out sufficiently, and that could not be repaired. It was not only because of the

Nazis but also because of the failure of Christians that such tremendous suffering had been caused through the German occupation in Poland, Holland, Czechoslovakia, France, Norway, Greece, and other countries. Repentance would have to express itself in willingness to bear each other's burden. One hope left was that a new day could be prepared by men who had the love of Christ in their hearts.

It was a vigorous message from the old fighting Niemoeller. He knew now what he had to say.

"The meeting turned out to be the most moving experience of reconciliation that could be imagined," said Dr. Samuel McCrea Cavert. "And it was Pastor Niemoeller who took the initiative and played the main role.

"To appreciate what happened at Stuttgart we must recall that after World War I a rather bitter discussion of 'war guilt' hung like a cloud over the relations of the churches of Germany and of other lands for several years. In contrast with this, the development at Stuttgart paved the way for an early understanding and cooperation which was of crucial ecumenical importance."

Martin Niemoeller then drafted a statement, which was adopted by the assembly, a statement that has become famous in the religious world as the Stuttgart Statement of Guilt. It read:

The Council of the Protestant Church in Germany, in its meeting on October 18 and 19 in Stuttgart, greets the representatives of the World Council of Churches.

We are all the more grateful for this visit as we know ourselves to be one with our people in a great company of suffering and in a great solidarity of guilt. With great pain do we say: Through us endless suffering has been brought to many peoples and countries. What we have often borne witness to before our congregations, that we now declare in the name of the whole church. True, we have struggled for many years in the name of Jesus Christ against a spirit which found its terrible expression in the National Socialist regime of violence, but we accuse ourselves for not witnessing more courageously, for not praying more faithfully, for not believing more joyously, and for not loving more ardently.

Now a new beginning is to be made in our churches. Grounded on the Holy Scriptures, directed with all earnestness toward the only Lord of the church, they now proceed to cleanse themselves from influences alien to the faith and to set themselves in order. Our hope is in the God of grace and mercy, that He will use our churches as His instruments and will give them authority to proclaim His Word and to make His will obeyed among ourselves and among our whole people.

That in this new beginning we may be aware of our whole-hearted unity with the other churches of the ecumenical fellowship fills us with deep joy.

We hope in God that through the common service of the church the spirit of violence and revenge which again today tends to become powerful may be brought under control in the whole world and that the spirit of peace and love wherein alone tortured humanity can find healing may gain the mastery.

So in an hour in which the whole world needs a new beginning we pray: *"Veni Creator Spiritus."*

The statement was signed by

Bishop Wurm	Pastor Niemoeller
Bishop Meiser	Landesoberkirchenrat Lilje
Superintendent Hahn	Superintendent Held
Bishop Dibelius	Pastor Niesel
Professor Smend	Dr. Heinemann
Pastor Asmussen	

"It took courage for the German Christian leaders to make such a statement," commented Dr. Cavert, "for it required little prescience to see that it would be resented by many Germans in the tense political situation of the months immediately following the war. The chief result, it is safe to say, was to give a powerful impetus to the forces of ecumenical cooperation."

"It was the beginning," said the Rev. Mr. Turner, "the beginning of dissolving war hate and ushering in reconciliation."

From Stuttgart the Niemoeller party continued to Berlin. On the way they picked up a Dr. Hannes Bartheau who wanted to go to Magdeburg in the Russian zone. Magdeburg had no medicine and many were sick. Bartheau had no papers but felt he should go there.

"Come along," Turner invited bravely.

At the check point at Helmstedt, Turner, in uniform, went in alone.

"Anyone else in the car with you?" asked the officer in charge, seeing that there was.

"Yes, Pastor Martin Niemoeller."

"You're kidding."

"I am not."

"Bring him in. I want to meet him."

The officer was very nice to Niemoeller. They had a pleasant conversation.

"Anyone else in the car?" he asked Turner, again looking over his shoulder.

"Yes, Mrs. Niemoeller."

"Anyone else?"

"Yes, a German doctor, a civilian."

Martin Niemoeller smiled at the officer, his famous, magic smile. The officer smiled back. But he felt he had to reprimand Turner somehow.

"I hope you do not continue to go around Germany taking unauthorized people into the Russian zone," he said severely.

As they drove on, a heavy fog set in. They stopped at

Magdeburg. The little doctor got out, carrying his two suitcases of medicine from the West. He disappeared into the fog. They drove on.

"I have never seen a person as depressed as Martin Niemoeller on this stage of the trip," Turner later recalled. "We drove through the Soviet zone. There it was, his country, occupied by the Russians."

There was an incentive for the Niemoellers to reach Berlin. Their son, Hermann, was there. Hermann had been a prisoner of the Russians at the end of the war but had managed to escape. He could not get back to Germany so he stayed in Bad Warmbrunn in Poland. There he was taken in by the kindly people of the town and especially by a man who had been a pastor in a Confessing Church there. He played the organ for the first church services, and stayed there from June until September, 1945. Then he had been able to get to Berlin. His arm required an operation as a result of battle injury, and he was still there.

But immediately upon arrival in Berlin Martin Niemoeller did a characteristic thing.

"Let's go to see Professor and Mrs. Bartning," he said impulsively. Bartning, an artist of renown, had been the lay chairman of the Dahlem congregation, a courageous man who had held the congregation together. Else was longing to see her son but she appreciated his generous impulse, so they went to see the Bartnings.

The Bartnings still lived in Dahlem in a small house. A bomb had gone directly through it and made a hole in the middle but it had not exploded. Mrs. Bartning, now a widow, still lives there.

Then they went to see Hermann. He was still very sick; the arm was badly inflamed. But it was a happy reunion. They visited their own home, which had been hit by a bomb and partially destroyed.

The congregation welcomed Niemoeller back, and he preached every night for a week. In his first sermon he told them how God called His Son to be sent into the wilderness. Now, his message followed, God's children are sent into the wilderness, which is Berlin.

Martin Niemoeller was in a state of exaltation during this period. But at the end of that week he had to face the painful fact that he probably would not be returning to Dahlem to live. Like many a returning serviceman, not protected by a special clause in the union contract, he found his place had been taken by someone who had stayed at home.

He bears absolutely no rancor at this state of affairs. It was quite understandable, he says reasonably. Bishop Dibelius was the general superintendent, having taken the title bishop so the Russians would know his standing. Another man had taken over the duties of pastor. There was no place open for him. But there are others who tell of the jealousy of one of the stay-at-home pastors and there are many who felt it was far from fair treatment.

Two scenes stood out in Turner's mind from that memorable week in Berlin. He took Niemoeller shortly after their arrival in the city to call on a sick layman in a hostel. When the pastor came out, he had a strange look on his face.

"Martin, what has happened?" asked Mrs. Niemoeller, who read her husband's face.

He told them the head nurse had related a story about Jutta, who, as a teen-age volunteer, had rolled bandages at the hospital during the war. They all kept going on their nerve in those hectic days, and one of the nurses had done something stupid. The head nurse had scolded her roughly. The next day Jutta saw the nurse going to church.

"Are you going to church?" she said. "But you cannot."

"Why not?"

Jutta quoted from the Sermon on the Mount, Matthew 5:23, 24:

"Therefore if thou bring thy gift to the altar, and there rememberest that thy brother hath ought against thee;

"Leave there thy gift before the altar, and go thy way; first be reconciled to thy brother, and then come and offer thy gift."

"I know it is possible to forgive," she added softly, "because Adolf Hitler has put my father in concentration camp and I have forgiven Adolf Hitler."

The nurse did so. And now she told the story. This evidence of the Christian witness in wartime on the part of his dead daughter touched Martin Niemoeller deeply.

They drove to Spandau to see a group of charitable institutions, a kind of miniature Bethel which had not been bombed. In one of the rooms on the second floor of the main building the first meeting of the board of the Confessing Church had been set up.

Turner stopped the car, and Martin Niemoeller jumped out. He started to run up the stairs, then remembered his wife, and stopped to wait for her.

The Niemoellers, side by side, walked into the meeting. No one present even knew they were in Berlin. There was complete silence. Then a sculptor, Wilhelm Gross, stood up. Gross, part Jewish, had been persecuted both as a Jew and as a Christian. There he stood, a gaunt, slender man with a haggard face. And then they all stood up. Of one accord, spontaneously, they began to sing:

"Nun danket alle Gott. . . ."

"Now thank we all our God. . . ."

21.

LIFE IN A CASTLE

THE trip back to Leoni was more dangerous than that to Berlin, because they had to pass the Russian check point instead of the American one, and also they had to smuggle the Niemoellers' son, Hermann, out with them.

Once again they reached Helmstedt and the check points. Beyond the Russian check point could be seen the British check point, a neatly painted building. Around the corner was the American check point. The Russians had only a guard rail. The guards emerged suddenly from behind the bushes.

Turner got out of the car and presented his papers. The guard looked at them, upside down.

Then he said, *"Du Okay. Deutsches in Wald,"* indicating that the Niemoellers were to be taken back into the woods.

For a moment Turner had a vision of a story reading, "When last seen, Pastor Martin Niemoeller was walking into the woods, surrounded by Russian guards." He decided to bluff it through. He offered the guard a cigarette. The guard took it. The answer was still, *"Nein."* No luck.

"Call your captain," Turner said. The guard called a sergeant. He, too, took a cigarette, looked at the papers upside down, and said, *"Nein. Du Okay. Deutsches nein."*

"Call your captain," Turner said. The sergeant called a lieutenant. The lieutenant said, *"Nein. Deutsches komm mitt."* Finally Turner got hold of the captain. The captain could read.

The Niemoellers' papers were in order, but the captain still shook his head.

Meanwhile, an American military truck came along. One of the men leaned out. "You in trouble, buddy?" he asked.

Turner said, "We sure are. Tell the American check point." Just then they saw a British sergeant swinging down the road, whistling as if he were headed for the river Kwai. Turner called to him.

"Hallo, there," he replied. "Don't think I can do much to help you. They're in a jolly nasty mood this afternoon."

"What are we going to do?" Turner asked.

The British sergeant turned around and blew a whistle.

To this day Turner does not know what the British sergeant intended to do, whether to call for help, send a special signal, or just try to impress the Russians. At any rate, the Russian captain stared for a minute, then flung up his arm—whing! The barrier went up. Shaking, Turner climbed into the car.

And then the motor wouldn't start.

After an agonizing minute or two it turned over. They drove on, grateful for their good luck. Not only had the Niemoellers been allowed to pass, but in the hubbub the Russians had completely missed their one vulnerable point—that they were smuggling Hermann across the lines.

They returned to Leoni but they could not stay there long. With the addition of Brigitte and Hermann there were nine people in three bedrooms. There was just not enough room.

"And so," Mrs. Niemoeller remarked casually, "we moved to a castle."

On his earlier trip to Frankfurt tentative plans had been made for Pastor Niemoeller to become head of the foreign affairs' office of the church. Now these plans had been completed and it was important that he be near Frankfurt. It was fortunate that at this very time they were offered lodgings in the castle of the Fuerst and Fuerstin (Prince and Princess) Ysenburg at Buedingen.

This was a friendship that began with a kindness of Martin Niemoeller's, one of the acts of human consideration which have won him many close admirers. The brother of the princess had been a confirmand at the Dahlem parish. In the middle of the church struggle in 1935 the prince and princess had asked Niemoeller to perform their marriage ceremony. This, in the face of all the state criticism of Niemoeller, was a courageous act, a vote of confidence from a family of nobility.

Later the prince yielded to pressure and became a member of the Nazi party. After the war Niemoeller spoke in favor of his liberation from prison, citing his earlier sentiments and his act of religious courage. In gratitude the prince offered him an apartment in the castle.

Buedingen was a convenient and comfortable sanctuary, but more than that, it had a charm and atmosphere all its own. The Niemoellers still return to visit there to enjoy the Old-World spell the thousand-year-old castle casts.

A fairy-tale castle, like a setting for *Sleeping Beauty,* Buedingen may be seen from a hilltop. It is surrounded by a moat where grass now grows, and then by a wall of red sandstone. The gate is called the Jerusalem Gate because it was built when one of the princes returned from the Crusades.

Just inside the grounds is a building called "the cottage," actually a small but beautifully furnished house set in the midst of a garden of rose trees. This is the home of Princess Mary von Ysenburg Buedingen who, with her husband, once lived in the castle. They had no children so they adopted their nephew, the present prince. He now lives in the castle with his family, and Princess Mary in the cottage with her sister.

A tall, pleasant-looking woman in tailored clothes, Princess Mary might easily be an English duchess. She has simplicity of manner but the courage of one born to responsibility and duty. During the war the little chapel at Buedingen was the local headquarters for the Confessing Church. Unlike her nephew, Princess Mary did not succumb to pressure but stayed aloof from the Nazi party.

There was a time during those years when no one in the community spoke to her on the street. Many who came to the church services in the chapel were threatened by the Nazis.

"If you are seen at the castle chapel again, you will not sell any iron," one businessman was told.

After the war was over the people in the community began greeting Princess Mary again, at first raising a hand in the Nazi form of salute, then, remembering how it used to be done, tipping the hat.

Down the hill from Princess Mary's cottage are more gates, another courtyard, another gate, an inner courtyard guarded by twin stone figures. Pastor Niemoeller loved the legend: When the stone men hear the bells at midnight they change places—when they hear the bells, that is.

Inside the inner courtyard are pyramid oaks, huge, many-branched trees. Doves flutter down from a dovecote. The atmosphere is so romantic that the visitor cannot help but look for the dove that will fly back into the tower and change into a beautiful princess.

Up a few steps from the entrance is the chapel door; over it, a cross with two figures of knights from the Crusades. Inside is a handsome room with carved wooden pews and a carved stone pulpit.

The entire palace is built in curves, one huge hall leading to another, each hall lined with books, portraits, crossed sabers. Off one of the halls is a small suite of rooms which the Niemoellers had: a living room, bedroom, a room for the children, a kitchen and bathroom combined. This room had been decorated with pictures of hunting scenes that annoyed housekeeper Dora. One day she came in looking happy. It was during de-nazification proceedings.

"I have just de-stagged the room," she said.

The Niemoellers came to the castle in November, 1945, and stayed until May, 1948. Life was not exactly easy. Food was hard to get. When Mrs. Niemoeller sent a CARE package to the castle among many packages for many other families, she was criticized for sending food to royalty.

There were problems at Buedingen, petty annoyances, disturbances. But the ancient spell is still there and the Niemoellers enjoy remembering the happy times like the first Christmas after the war.

It was an austere Christmas. Spartan economy prevailed. But they did their best to keep up the traditions.

The Rev. Mr. Turner came to spend Christmas with his friends. Presents were exchanged even though no one had much to give. But as is the custom at German Christmas celebrations each person had a little table with his gifts on it.

There was a service in the chapel, and the children sang Christmas carols. For Christmas dinner, miraculously enough, there was a chicken.

"The rooms were cold," Turner later summed up his remembrances, "but where the Niemoeller family celebrated Christmas, there was warmth."

22.

THE GUILT EXISTS

THE guilt of the German people exists, even if there were no other guilt than that of the six million clay urns containing the ashes of burned Jews from all over Europe."

These were strong words that Martin Niemoeller spoke and few Germans were conditioned to accept them. The German people were in rags in those years of 1945 and 1946. ("I am administering communion again," a pastor wrote to American friends, "but my parishioners do not know that under my trousers I have no underwear.") Newborn babies were wrapped in newspapers in lieu of clothes. No one had enough to eat. The houses still standing often lacked windowpanes. And the refugees poured through the land in an endless, weary stream.

"Alles kaput," were the words that greeted every traveler in Germany. All was finished, wrecked, over.

Niemoeller told them it was they themselves, not the enemy, who was responsible.

"Nobody wants to take the responsibility of the guilt," Niemoeller said in one of his early sermons. "No one of our German people is guilty. Everybody shoves the guilt off on his neighbor. The local official says: I was only a little man, the whole guilt lies with you, Herr local commander; and he, in turn says, I did not wrong anybody; I only obeyed orders.

The whole guilt lies with you, you of the Gestapo. But the latter don't want it either, and finally everything lands on Himmler and Hitler. These are the greatest sinners, who cannot throw the guilt on others any more, even if they did try to do so before their deaths. Can it disappear into thin air this way? The guilt exists, there is no doubt about it."

It was not only those outside the church whom he blamed. What would have happened, he asked, if all the Evangelical communities in 1933 and 1934 had stood up to the Nazis?

"I can imagine," he surmised, "that thirty to forty thousand Evangelical Christians would have been shortened by a head, but I can also imagine that we would have thus saved thirty to forty millions of lives, for this is the price that we now have to pay."

It was not a popular message. Even his friends sighed their familiar, "Oh, Martin, do you have to say it just that way?" As for the rank and file of the German people, they rejected it flatly. Such headlines as "Protestant Church Acknowledges Germany's War Guilt" and "Niemoeller Accuses Germans of Collective Guilt" brought forth resentment. In vain Niemoeller protested that he had not used the phrase "collective guilt," that he preferred "collective responsibility." But "collective guilt" was the tag given his belief by the newspapers and "collective guilt" it remained.

In a letter to a friend, written in November, 1945, Pastor Niemoeller endeavored to explain precisely what it was he was trying to say.

Never have I declared that all the German people, indiscriminately and without exception, are responsible and guilty of the crimes of the Nazis, but again and again I have said that we have no right to blame everything on the bad Nazis and pretend that we are without fault or guilt.

Of course we are not all murderers and thieves and sadists

but we have done little or nothing to put a stop to the corruption, and particularly we, meaning the church, have failed. We have known about the wrong and the right way and we have let men follow the ways of corruption without warning. I have not excluded myself from this guilt. I have even included myself explicitly for I, too, was silent when I should have spoken. If we do not turn about and admit in our hearts that we have taken the wrong way for reasons of fear and faithlessness, then the burden will remain upon us.

Even if we begin to list the sins of the others to them, now that we have filled a world with agony and blood and corpses, with ruin and desolation, then I can only say that all of it is but a particle compared to the load which we have on our consciences. And I say this after I have been to Berlin for twelve days where there is hardly a woman who has not been disgraced and where death walks the streets in a manner the world has never seen before—*except in Poland and Czechoslovakia and western Russia.*

It was not a welcome message for the German people but it had a great effect on the outside world. It has often been pointed out by way of comparison that after World War I it was seven years before contacts with churches in Germany were restored. But by February, 1946, less than ten months after the end of the war in Europe, Bishop Wurm and Pastor Niemoeller were in Geneva attending a meeting of the Provisional Committee for the World Council of Churches with the highest Protestant representatives of France, Norway, Holland, England, and America.

It was a moving occasion. During a service at the cathedral Bishop Berggrav of Norway told how he had received word in prison that the archbishop of Canterbury was praying for him. Then Niemoeller, who spoke in French on this occasion, told how his aged father had reported to him in prison that the archbishop of Canterbury was praying for him. There was the archbishop sitting just below the pulpit. Afterwards, Henry

Smith Leiper presented Niemoeller to him and they embraced like long-lost brothers.

Others at that historic meeting, men from countries ravaged by the Nazis, paid tribute to Niemoeller. When the delegate from China, carried away by the occasion, disregarded his limit and cut the bishop of Copenhagen and Niemoeller down to twelve minutes, the Danish bishop in a single sentence deferred to Niemoeller.

The Stuttgart Declaration of Guilt played its part at this meeting in laying a foundation for a full and creative sharing of the German Church in the World Council of Churches which came into being shortly thereafter.

Germans, disagreeing or not with him, came to hear Niemoeller. He was a speaker in great demand at churches, universities, public meetings. After the family moved to Buedingen, he began to travel as much as roads would permit and to speak and preach. In the beginning he drove his own car. Then one day he struggled for an hour to get the snow chains off the car and fell over, exhausted. The next day he hired a driver and has had one ever since.

Hermann, his eldest living son, often accompanied him on these trips. It was in the days when it was hard to get food but everyone made a special effort to serve good meals for the visiting pastor. Pastor Niemoeller often is indifferent to food but Hermann was always hungry. They would return from a journey and "Mutti" Niemoeller would ask how things had gone. Hermann's regular report was, "Father worked, the driver drove, and I ate."

Some meetings were soberly received, some excited argument or discussion. After all, "We didn't know," people tried to tell the pastor. Or, "If we had known, what could we have done?" Some meetings ended in near riots with shouting and heckling. Especially was this true at student meeting places.

Once at a meeting at Siegen, in Westphalia, Niemoeller spoke in a tunnel hollowed out of a mountain for a bomb shelter. The angry crowd threw stones at him as he left.

"The Stuttgart statement and the things Martin said were misinterpreted over and over," said his friend, Heinz Kloppenburg. "The statement only said we Christians confess we were not brave enough or gallant enough to trust in the Lord. The press said Niemoeller says Germans are guilty of all the terrible crimes the Nazis committed. Many people said, 'Here is a churchman who calls us criminals.' Others said, 'Martin dirties his own nest.' And they were all wrong. But the one thing which people find hardest to swallow is absolute honesty."

Niemoeller criticized the occupation forces as relentlessly as he had criticized the Nazis and his fellow men. In April, 1946, he made headlines when he said the delay of the Allied powers to determine Germany's future was the greatest obstacle to destroying the last trace of nazism, re-educating German youth, and shortening the period of military occupation.

"We can tell the young Germans our ideals but we cannot give them the aim, the goal to work for," he said. "If we could tell what the boundaries of Germany would be—the territorial, economic, and other boundaries—it would be different. We must be able to give youth some picture of what to live for and what to work for. The moment we give them something to aim at, the dangers of National Socialism will be gone forever. Some younger Germans," he added, "are clinging to National Socialism as a man in the open sea clings to a plank, not because it is a very strong plank, but because it is all he has. The young people just do not see the other plank. They must be shown something that makes democracy alluring."

In the fall of 1946 came the Nuremberg Trials and Niemoeller directed sharp criticism at their conduct. He approved the acquittal of Hjalmar Schacht and Franz von Papen but not that of Hans Fritzsche, whom he considered a "convinced Nazi." And he made old friends furious when he did not speak up for some of his own former comrades in arms. In a speech to students at Erlangen he said of the Nuremberg Trials and of some of his old comrades in arms from World War I: "There sits Raeder, my one-time commanding officer, and Doenitz, my one-time shipmate. From 1942 to 1946 these men signed orders to which every officer would have refused to subscribe as short a time ago as 1918. The ethical standards of a mere twenty years ago had rapidly disappeared. We had no longer any scruples of conscience. They were not considered up to date. To obey one's conscience meant to lay down one's life.

"People said during these last twelve years, 'We are strong and manly men. We can take the responsibility for what we do. Religion is just for old women.' But look at these manly men. They made not only the German people but all the nations of Europe bear the consequences of their actions."

Looking back today on the Nuremberg Trials, Martin Niemoeller criticizes them only because they took too long and were one-sided.

"I thought England, America, France, and Russia should have been punished, too," he says. "But the victor has never made aggression, only defended. You hang a thief when he has stolen something that belongs to you but when you yourself steal, you are not subject to any judgment."

He continued to hammer away at guilt. In October, 1946, *Tagesspiegel,* an American licensed Berlin newspaper, quoted a paragraph from a sermon delivered in a Berlin church:

"The guilt question is not discussed today—it is avoided," he said. "So far we have not taken seriously the conceptions of guilt and atonement. We were dreaming when we thought guilt belonged to the past. When, however, in the midst of a Christian people six million persons are deliberately murdered

23.

MEETING AMERICAN FRIENDS

AGAIN the Naples press conference was to rise
up and haunt Niemoeller. In June, 1946, Bishop G. Bromley
Oxnam invited him to come to the United States and make a
series of appearances under the sponsorship of the Federal
Council of Churches, the body that later came to be the
National Council of Churches. The trip had to be postponed
until winter, but finally, on December 2, 1946, Niemoeller
left by plane from Berlin for New York. Because the Reverend
Ewart Turner was the American he knew best, he asked him
to be his traveling companion. He was met in New York by
Turner, Eleanor Kent Browne, who had arranged his American tour, and Dr. Fritz Bardi, one-time Reichstag member.
To reporters who met the plane he said:

"The Christian Church exists as a bond between the peoples
of this world. Although the material needs are many, the
fundamental malady of the world is a spiritual one and our
fundamental cure must be a spiritual one.

"The opportunity and responsibility of the Christian church
today on the continent of Europe are tremendous. We must
not fail the youth of the war-torn countries who are looking
for some vital faith and some living hope."

This was Martin Niemoeller, the *hausvater,* speaking, the pastor concerned with his flock, the father with his children.

The auspicious beginning of the trip was soon marred. On December 4 Martin Niemoeller, the political figure, was attacked by Mrs. Eleanor Roosevelt in her column, "My Day."

I understand that Dr. Niemoeller has stated in the past that he was against the Nazis because of what they did to the Church but that he had no quarrel with them politically. And I think I remember reading a report that when his country went to war, he offered his services for submarine work in the Navy.

One may applaud his bravery and his devotion to his church but one can hardly applaud his attitude on the Nazi politics and I cannot quite see why we should be asked to listen to his lectures. I am sure he is a good man according to his lights but his lights are not those of the people of the United States who did not like the Hitler political doctrines.

There were several replies to this attack. One was the formal reply of the Federal Council of the Churches of Christ in America which sent a telegram, signed by Bishop Oxnam:

Deeply regret the misinformation on which your remarks about Pastor Niemoeller in your column are based. The record clearly shows that he repeatedly spoke against the political aims of the Nazis. As early as 1933 he was forbidden to preach as a result of his speaking against Hitler's racialistic program.

We urge you to correct erroneous impression created by your column and give recognition to the fact that he was as courageous in his stand against Nazis politics long before our own country was alert to the danger.

Another answer came from David L. Ostergren, the chaplain who met and talked with Niemoeller at Naples. He related some of the results of this talk in "An Open Letter on Pastor Niemoeller," dated December 6, and explained how he felt Niemoeller's point of view had been distorted by the press.

Still another spirited defense of Niemoeller appeared in *The Christian Century* for January 15, 1947. Entitled, "Play Fair with Niemoeller!" it read in part:

What *do* the people of the United States owe Pastor Martin Niemoeller, who is now lecturing in this country? More than most of us realize. The least we can give him is a fair hearing, although some would deny him that. When Niemoeller arrived in this land to address the Federal Council of Churches, Mrs. Eleanor Roosevelt said, "I cannot quite see why we should be asked to listen to his lectures." The Federal Council could see why. It replied that this minister of the Evangelical Church in Germany had earned the right to address the court of American public opinion. If he had not earned it in eight years spent in the Dachau and Sachsenhausen concentration camps, then the Council invited consideration of his earlier anti-Nazi record. "As early as 1933 he was forbidden to preach as a result of his speaking against Hitler's racialistic program," it said.

The American people are indebted to Pastor Niemoeller for taking his stand against tyranny with such fortitude that he became to millions in all lands the symbol of courage in the fight for freedom. Why not repay to Hitler's most famous prisoner a little of the debt we owe to many hundred thousand resolute Germans and citizens of other nations who bore the brunt of the first costly resistance to the Nazis?

The Christian Century further pointed out that even though the policy of the United States was following a "get-tough-with-Germany" trend, it was necessary to discriminate between Germans who understand and sympathize with democratic aims and those who do not.

In taking its stand for such discrimination, it pointed out that, "during the war we promised we would do that in broadcasts heard by Germans who risked their lives to listen

to the Allied radio." It concluded with an appeal for fair
play for Niemoeller—"an ambassador of reconciliation for
the ecumenical church."

Mrs. Roosevelt never quite retracted, although she back-
tracked a little. In a later column she wrote:

"We know that Pastor Niemoeller himself, because of his
religious stand, suffered in Hitler's concentration camp." However, she added, that in her opinion "Germans who are public
figures in any field should not come to our shores at the present
time unless they have a record of having fought the Nazi
policies every step of the way, and if that was the case, I fear
they would not be alive to come here today."

With this controversial send-off the tour got under way.
The first speech was scheduled for Seattle, where the Federal
Council was holding its annual meeting. The plane failed to
make connections at Spokane and was temporarily grounded
but the Niemoellers arrived on split-second timing at the First
Presbyterian Church in Seattle, where 3,900 people waited.
Mayor William Devin was there and Bishop Oxnam presided.

Speaking on "The Faith That Sustained Me," Martin Niemoeller made two points: (1) that Hitler's failure to replace
Christianity with his own ideology proved that the true word
of God cannot be defeated by any temporal power; and (2)
that a church unity cutting across nations and denominations
is the intent of God and the one real assurance of the church's
future.

Commented a Seattle newspaper: "He is indeed a welcome
guest. Germans of his sort are the hope of Germany."

And it was a Seattle reporter who furnished a line repeated
many times. He left the church, shaking his head and saying
sadly, "Think of a man spending eight years in a concentration
camp and not having anything to talk about except Jesus
Christ."

Because of the rigorous nature of the tour of fifty-two cities and Niemoeller's still fragile state of health, Turner had been firm about scheduling press conferences. Only four were set up, in Seattle, Atlanta, Chicago, and New York. This did not make the press very happy but it lightened the load for the Niemoellers. Even so the pace was grueling.

From Seattle they went to Portland where 5,000 came to hear Niemoeller. In San Jose, California, they crowded the church, sitting on the steps leading to the altar. There was a mix-up between the date in Portland and one in San Francisco, both having been scheduled for the same day, but luckily they were able to cancel a second Portland date and move on.

In Portland, the pastor had heart palpitations and a refugee doctor who had known him in Dahlem was called in. The doctor positively forbade Niemoeller to talk that night but Niemoeller spoke anyway.

By the time they reached Los Angeles, Turner was reeling under the strain. A pastor friend there came to the rescue with an offer to lend his secretary, on vacation with pay from the church. The secretary, Gladys Baugus, joined the tour and was a tremendous help.

The tour continued. To Phoenix, to Tucson, where the pastor visited the Cabot chapel, a former garage converted into a chapel, where students had written letters to Hitler asking for Niemoeller's release.

On to Fort Worth, Kansas City, St. Paul, Minneapolis, Cedar Rapids, Davenport, Chicago. There the German manager of the Blackstone Hotel welcomed the Niemoellers with flowers and fruit, and a newspaper editorial said, "Years may come and go before the approximately 3,000 fortunate persons who were there again hear a religious force as moving as the voice of Martin Niemoeller."

On to Atlanta, where Niemoeller met Bishop Arthur J. Moore, who had had a date to have tea with him in Berlin the day he was arrested. In Richmond, Virginia, he renewed acquaintance with student Thomas Lovelace, who had been a corporal at the hotel in Naples. At Louisville, Kentucky, Mrs. Marlene Maertens, the widow of his classmate Erhard Maertens, introduced him to a responsive crowd.

In St. Louis Niemoeller visited Eden Seminary which had conferred his first honorary doctorate on him during the days of the church struggle. Back to Chicago again, where Dr. Louis Binstock of Temple Sholom devoted a sermon to him.

"Dr. Niemoeller is not yet ready for the role of a hero or a martyr," said Dr. Binstock, "but he has a quality of honesty that shines right through his eyes and he has both courage and true bravery."

From Detroit they went to New York and Brooklyn and Newark, back west to Indianapolis and a crowd of 11,000, to Columbus, Cleveland, Oberlin, Dayton, Cincinnati. In each town he was greeted by friends from his former parish, and in each town he made new friends. The Rev. Mr. Turner noticed one significant gesture that was evident again and again.

"Time after time," he said, "people would line up as he went out to the car and reach over and touch him."

There was little opposition despite the stormy start of the trip. There was an objection to the ruling against press conferences in Detroit, a small protest parade in Dayton, Ohio, a move to prevent his speaking in Hartford, Connecticut. A Hartford newspaper editorial commented that "People who oppose his appearance in Hartford seem to have a strange idea of the meaning of free speech."

The tour rolled on—to Covington, Grand Rapids, Gettysburg, Washington, Hartford, Worcester, Massachusetts, Schenectady, Albany, Buffalo, Rochester, Toronto, and, finally, on March 11, back to New York.

Niemoeller had spoken on many subjects, on the guilt of the German people, on the experiences of the church in Germany, on the hopes of the future. In New York he spoke for a just peace, stating that "no peace built on vengeance can last."

Before he left, he did one more thing in an effort to help conditions in postwar Germany. He had his friend, the Rev. Frederick J. Forell, introduce a letter he had written into the *Congressional Record*. A plea for food packages, it concluded, "You may become God's messenger of Christ's love and help people to die at least in peace, reconciled with earthly suffering and grief. . . . May God bless you, dear Brother Forell, and all you do in order to mitigate the suffering of people who have paid more than an eye for an eye and a tooth for a tooth for their credulity in a new savior and may our one-and-only Saviour have mercy on us."

When Mr. Turner accompanied the Niemoellers to the airport in New York, he asked the pastor what he thought his message would be from now on.

Niemoeller considered a moment and then gave a careful and direct answer, as he does to every serious question.

"From now on," he said, "I think a good part of my life will be given to an attempt to build a bridge between the East and the West. This grows out of a simple conviction that I have that if there is no bridge between East and West, then World War III will be inevitable."

24.

ECUMENICAL SPIRIT GROWS

THERE are many Lutheran bishops who would have preferred a nice chapel in Dachau in memory of Martin Niemoeller where they could have gone in silent prayer instead of having him among them as a living Christian."

This statement, attributed to Karl Barth, is widely quoted by friends and admirers of Martin Niemoeller as descriptive of the attitude of those German churchmen who would have preferred a dead hero to a living and omnipresent thorn in their sides.

These same admirers, the ones who look on Niemoeller as a prophet, readily admit that he is a prophet without adequate honor in his own country, at least in that part of Germany now under Western control. Many of them are also of the opinion that he did not get fair recognition from his own church after the war.

"Martin is too modern to be able to reach those people who love security and who consider a conservative attitude the summit of piety," his brother Wilhelm has said.

"You do not appreciate what my husband has done," Else Niemoeller put it much more bluntly, in a conversation with Bishop Dibelius between sessions of the Treysa conference.

It was at the Treysa conference, the first postwar meeting of German Protestants in August, 1945, that the old hostilities flared up. And while Niemoeller made a dramatic impression with his call for repentance, it was at Treysa that it became apparent that postwar control of the church would be taken over by the conservatives, the middle-of-the-roaders, the neutrals, and in some instances by those who had "sat it out."

Characteristically, Niemoeller himself does not give any indication that he experienced disappointment because the church failed to welcome him back as their leader.

"I was young at the time, just fifty-three," he has said, looking back on the church reorganization. "There were other leading churchmen who took precedence over me. Oh, I do remember being a little disappointed when I found I could not go back to Berlin."

Niemoeller's attitude might be explained by his modesty, or even by his customary indifference to worldly honor. Certainly there is no worldly honor he would consider worth playing politics for. But there are others who think he was not badly treated by the church. An outstanding American theological seminarian replied to the question of injustice to Niemoeller rather testily with the statement, "Being in concentration camp doesn't qualify one for being head of the church." And Niemoeller's son, Hermann, finds it quite understandable that his father was not given a high position.

"He is too extraordinary to be really liked or even appreciated by the majority of the church leaders," he said. "He's much too uncomfortable a person to be around. If some principle is at stake, he doesn't care what the results will be. In order to achieve a high office, he would have had to be very diplomatic —something he just couldn't do."

Certainly he was not diplomatic in those early postwar days. For one thing, he kept harping on that unpleasant subject of guilt.

"As if we could have done anything about it," an annoyed woman said to Niemoeller's friend, Marlene Maertens.

"This was the same woman," Mrs. Maertens recalled dryly,

"who once said to me during the Jewish persecution, 'It was really too awful. They were dragging the Jews through the streets under my very windows. I finally had to close the shutters to keep from hearing their screams.' "

Besides the subject of guilt there was a genuine difference of opinion on subjects temporal and theological. An early debate occurred on the subject of church taxes. The Confessing Church, cut off from tax support in Hitler's time, had been able to exist on free-will offerings, and Niemoeller often voiced the opinion that this form of support, such as sustains churches in America, would be a step forward in revitalizing churches in Germany. As has been pointed out before, the paradox of the German church is its strong financial support by the majority—95 per cent of the citizens willingly pay a church tax to the Catholic or Protestant church organization—and the poor support in attendance and activity, with less than 10 per cent of the population responsibly identified with the church. A German is born with his church membership, expects to be rendered the traditional services of baptism, marriage, and burial, but rarely belongs to a church in the sense Americans belong. Consequently, rule is also by the few.

"Today the church is the most undemocratic thing in all of Germany," Niemoeller said several months after Treysa. "My whole aim is to bring revival out of the local parish."

Other differences sprang from Niemoeller's liberal attitude toward church differences in dogma. Long a proponent of a German Evangelical church rather than three Evangelical churches in Germany, Niemoeller becomes impatient when the Lutherans and the Calvinists argue their historic differences on the Lord's Supper.

Hermann Niemoeller went with his father to Heidelberg in 1947 to visit a professor of theology, a theologian of orthodox Lutheran background.

"I couldn't help noticing the divergence of their theological thinking," Hermann observed later. "My father could not be concerned about the niceties. The question of the Holy Supper, dating back to the sixteenth and seventeenth centuries, simply didn't seem important to him any more. He was becoming too ecumenical-minded."

And here lies the key to much of the discomfort many German churchmen felt around Martin Niemoeller. He was no longer of them but of the world. Shortly after the Stuttgart meeting he had attended the provisional committee meeting of the World Council of Churches in Geneva. He cut quite a figure at the Amsterdam Conference which established the Council. He had lectured in America. Why was he gallivanting around to other countries instead of tending to his knitting at home?

"When Martin Niemoeller went into the concentration camp he was a German nationalist," Ewart Turner once said. "When he came out he was on the way to being a world church leader."

Turner believes that three things accomplished this.

First of all, in concentration camp he was forced to be a shepherd of souls for persons of many religious faiths. In Sachsenhausen he read mass to the priest-gardener and seriously considered the possibility of adopting the Catholic faith. In Dachau he continued his inquiry into Catholicism and attempted to explain Protestantism to the three priests interned with him.

The second thing that led him along the ecumenical path was the immediate reception given him by world church leaders. Many have pointed out that it was Niemoeller's very existence and example which were responsible for the attitude of the rest of the world toward the German churches. In turn, he was impressed by the friendliness of the foreign churchmen he met.

And finally, the trip to America formed his ecumenical

spirit. The German EKID recognized this when they made him the head of their foreign office. This was his first church position. Then in October, 1947, he became president of the church in Hesse and Nassau. The two positions were neither conflicting nor mutually exclusive, though many felt he was spending too much time on his foreign interests and resented it.

These three things, his absolute honesty and lack of diplomacy, his indifferences to theological niceties, and his one-world spirit, were enough to make him unpopular with many. But then came a series of bombshells in the form of his sharp criticisms of government policy. Niemoeller was starting to practice what he preached, that the church should have a voice in the affairs of the world. This many German Protestants could not accept.

"The old system was wrong," one churchman admitted. "The church should raise its voice now and then. But Niemoeller goes too far. He wants the church to have something to say about everything. He wants the government to consult him before each decision."

One of the first acts of the occupation forces criticized by Niemoeller was de-nazification. Many others of the clergy objected to indiscriminate de-nazification and for good reason. Stewart Herman in *Rebirth of the German Church* gives a graphic illustration of the kind of thing that could and did happen. He writes:

Pastor X knew two teachers. Teacher number one joined the Party early and stayed in, although he came to realize that he had made a mistake. He joined the Confessing Church and for years fought its battles at great risk to himself and his family. His children were brought up and educated in a thoroughly Christian fashion. This man was now barred from teaching. Teacher number two never joined the Party but was in complete sympathy with Nazi ideas. He even resigned from the church, ridiculed it, and prevented his children from receiving Christian instruction. This man was not only reinstated in his position, but he became a teacher of religion.

As a result of such inequity, wrote Herman, "Democracy was being compared with nazism and there was some tendency in the western zones to turn to communism."

"If," said Martin Niemoeller, "the people could really see democracy at work, the church would more easily accomplish its task of moral and spiritual rehabilitation."

On February 2, 1948, Martin Niemoeller released a letter to be read from all the pulpits in Hesse and Nassau, condemning the American policy of indiscriminate de-nazification and forbidding his pastors to take any part in it, as judges or witnesses.

"Our people have not been led along the path of atonement but down the road to reprisal," he said, "and the new seed of hatred which has been sown has grown profusely."

In an interview in May, he further clarified his stand by stating that he thought de-nazification should have been left to the churches, not to a military government. You cannot "change an ideology by laws," he said. "A deep ideological change can come about only through the Gospel and the grace of the Holy Spirit."

Looking back on that era today, Niemoeller feels he was right in criticizing de-nazification and that its basic principles were wrong.

"It all hinged on this question," he said. " 'Could one punish a man for his convictions as long as he did no criminal thing?' The occupation forces' methods made people wonder if they had not exchanged one arbitrary government for another. People began to think that there were no moral laws, only a moral law dependent on power. De-nazification was a source of bribery and corruption. You had a good friend among the Americans or British or French and you were safe. The thieves were hanged and the big shots went free. These things had a shattering effect on public morale."

Other German churchmen criticized de-nazification, too, among them Bishops Hans Lilje of Hannover and Hans Meiser of Bavaria, but it was Niemoeller's criticisms that made headlines in the United States and which had repercussions.

In January, 1949, the EKID synod met. Bishop Wurm being ill, Niemoeller presided as next in command. It was a foregone conclusion that a new chairman would be elected and Niemoeller was considered by many to be a likely candidate. But he had alienated too many groups by his outspoken criticisms. Bishop Dibelius was elected chairman. Niemoeller was not even re-elected to his post as deputy chairman. Instead, Bishop Lilje replaced him. It was, he admitted later, "rather disappointing."

Martin Niemoeller was not put aside entirely. He remained a member of the EKID council and president of the Church Foreign Office. However, at the July, 1949, meeting there was criticism by some of the conservative Lutheran groups concerning his conduct of that office. It was only a murmur, but it was to grow.

The year 1949 was not all discord. Niemoeller's attendance at the World Council of Churches meeting in Amsterdam was a great success. Asked to speak to 10,000 Dutch youths in a stadium meeting, he was told he could speak in German although up to that time there had been a strict rule against the use of German in any public addresses. When he finished, they gave him a tremendous ovation.

In the fall of the year another pleasant experience transcended bickering at home. An Australian, Lesleigh Werry, had read of Martin Niemoeller when he was a soldier fighting on the field and had promised himself that someday he would bring this man to Australia. When he returned home he made plans to do just that. Friends laughed at him because he had no funds to arrange such a tour. Nevertheless, he wrote to Niemoeller, who said he would be happy to come provided transportation could be arranged for him and his wife. Werry went to a prominent Brisbane businessman who agreed to underwrite the trip.

Meetings were arranged through the archbishop of Sidney. The tour was led by Werry and Jim Duffacy. "Faith Triumphant" was its theme. With an English singer, Jacques Hopkins, the group made appearances at every major city and town in Australia, New Zealand, and Tasmania. The Niemoellers often get out a scrapbook of snapshots assembled by their Australian friends. The pictures show Mrs. Niemoeller with a koala bear; Niemoeller, pipe in mouth, typewriter on lap, composing one of his sermons; welcoming crowds, individuals who became new friends. They like to relive the happy memories of August 24 to November 20, 1949.

It was a welcome respite. Then they returned to Germany and more conflict.

25.

REARMAMENT AND REUNIFICATION

It was a beautiful, sunny July day at the Bossey near Geneva, Switzerland, the World Council of Churches conference center. A group of American pastors were visiting with Martin Niemoeller and had walked away from the château to sit in the shade of a cluster of trees for an informal talk. They asked him if he had a message for them to take back to their congregations. One of the pastors, the Rev. Dr. Ervine Inglis of the First Congregational Church of Webster Groves, Missouri, remembers the words vividly because they made such a profound impression on him.

"Go back to your churches," Pastor Niemoeller said, "and use every bit of influence you have to prevent your country from compelling us to arm. We don't want to arm. We've had all we want of arms. We Germans know we are a good people. We are leaders who, in some respects, cannot be matched in Europe—until we get a gun in our hands and we go crazy. We are too susceptible to leadership. We Germans cannot stand to be armed. If you compel us to arm, the day will come when we will rip the world to pieces again."

The time was July, 1953, but it was neither the first nor the last time that Martin Niemoeller spoke eloquently against the rearming of western Germany. Reunification, rearmament, and Russia—these are the three R's which have kept Martin Niemoeller in political hot water for the past decade. He has made dire predictions and prognostications concerning all three. Some of them have come true.

One of Niemoeller's predictions was that rearmament would ruin chances of reunification for a long time to come. At least, as of 1959, he seems to be right.

"There was a chance when the question of rearmament was at stake, before the H-bomb, when the Russians were afraid of the German soldiers," Niemoeller said. "We might have bargained with them then—a unified Germany in place of a rearmed Germany. The experiment never was made and two years later the whole transaction was no longer possible.

"Today it makes no difference how many soldiers there are in Germany because we're not going to fight with soldiers but with atomic weapons. Whether there are 100,000 soldiers more or less doesn't matter to the Russians now. We have nothing to barter."

Reunification is a touchy subject with the West German government. The effects of the division of Germany touch every family as painfully as if the United States were split along the Mississippi River, relatives in Illinois separated from those in Missouri. Aside from the natural desire of any country to be united, division brings about the vexing, frustrating problem of interrupted transportation and correspondence.

Every American visitor to Germany is made aware of the contrast by going from prosperous, brightly lighted West Berlin by guarded bus tour through the dreary, still-rubble-strewn, almost empty streets of East Berlin. Church and welfare visitors have had ample opportunity to see the refugees, the *fluechtlinge* escapees, who stream over daily by the hundreds from the East Zone, leaving business, property, possessions, to start life anew in the West. Western Germany is dotted with refugee screening centers, camps, schools. The Protestant welfare agency Hilfswerk and its Catholic counterpart Caritas do a major part of their work with refugees.

And the desire for reunification is a constant ache in the German heart.

"Adenauer never really moved a finger in order to find out under what conditions reunification would be made," Niemoeller charged. "He said it must be. He prophesied it would be. He said wait a little longer. We are still waiting."

Soon after he returned from Australia, Niemoeller made headlines in the American press in an interview with reporter Marguerite Higgins on reunification. As usual when he is interviewed by someone with a flair for the pointed question, he could not resist the rapier answer.

The question was, "Do you think that in order to reunite East and West Germany most Germans would be prepared to pay the price of having a communist regime?"

Miss Higgins reported that Niemoeller answered, "Yes," without hesitation, and went on to say, "Given the alternative of a continued split in Germany or the prospect of reuniting the country under a foreign dictatorship—even that of Russia —the Germans would prefer to take the risk of communism. They would feel that they would have more chance of surviving as a nation under those circumstances."

Asked if he did not think he would be liquidated if the Communists took over, he replied airily, "Oh, it's quite probable. Quite probable."

A typical American headline read, "Niemoeller for United Germany Even at Cost of Control by Reds," which was not precisely what the story said. And later Niemoeller said the entire quote had been blown up out of context. What he had really meant, he clarified, was that if the German people were ever forced to the extremity of making a choice between permanent division or communist control, they might make the desperate decision in favor of communism, but he doubted and denied that this choice was necessary. It is a good example of his unparalleled genius for putting his foot in his mouth in press interviews.

What he also said at the time, although it did not lend itself to headlines, was this:

"Unless the U.N. takes over Germany, restoring its unity and ending the feud between Russia and the West, both Germany and Europe are finished."

Germany he likened to a family that has been split up.

"A family prefers to remain together. Even if it has been enslaved, members of the family prefer to remain in bondage rather than to leave one part of the family to its fate while the other enjoys freedom."

Germany, he said, was in a state of "political nihilism" with "all the hope of 1945 gone." The quarrel between East and West had made a "sensible development of policy in Germany impossible." He further stated that he found no enthusiasm for militarism and not a single person he talked to wanted "to carry a gun or has shown anything but opposition to the idea of a German army."

In January, 1950, in an open letter to the minister of the interior of the Bonn government, Niemoeller said:

"The only hope, if the division of Germany is not to lead to a third world war, is for the U.N. to take over all the occupation and administer the country as a once-more-united nation.

"There can be no peace in Europe as long as the German people do not have peace."

In the fall of 1950 another open letter, this one signed by the Brethren Council of the Confessing Church but accompanied by a personal letter from Niemoeller to Adenauer, charged that the Bonn government was attempting to revive militarism. The charge grew out of a letter from Lieutenant General Paul Mahlmann to a friend who knew Niemoeller, in which the general referred to the formation of German troop units. The Bonn government denied that rearmament was being planned. These were only labor battalions intended to guard United States army stores, they said. However, Eugen Gerstenmaier, founder and director of the Protestant Hilfswerk before he became head of the Bundestag, had called rearmament "our inescapable Christian responsibility."

Commented *The Christian Century* editorially, "Martin Niemoeller has as sure an instinct as had Martin Luther for picking out the hot spots in his nation's affairs and plunging into them."

For this criticism of the government, Niemoeller was rebuked by the EKID, but mildly. However, Bishop Dibelius at the next synod meeting made it plain that he did not agree by warning against "secularization," and making it clear that he thought rearmament should be left to the state, not the church.

Besides the differences of opinion with Western political forces on reunification and rearmament came the charge that Niemoeller was defending Communists. In June, 1950, the EKID, investigating his speeches, came up with such quotations as:

"Whoever condemns the Communists because of their ideology is anti-Christ.

"Communists are called to be the children of God.

"Christ might say today, 'The Communists and the harlots may go to heaven before you do.'

"It is not necessary to go to war against communism to save the Christian church and Christianity. . . . It is un-Christian to conduct a war for the maintenance of the Christian Church, because the church does not need to be saved. The church is not afraid of bolshevism as it was not afraid of the Nazis.

"The church has to serve the Communists as well as all human beings. While the church rejects communism as a creed just as it rejects all creeds, communism must and can only be fought and defeated with spiritual weapons. All other powers will fail."

Niemoeller visits East Germany as if no barrier existed. His appearances at churches in the East Zone are numerous, and he is a welcome guest, feted and fussed over.

There are those who contend that Niemoeller is vulnerable on one point—that he minimizes the persecution of the Protestant churches in the East Zone. Niemoeller, on his side, is sharp in his criticism of the West's attitude in the war of nerves and the church struggle which began in 1953 and has gone on with increasing rancor ever since.

Every church visitor to Germany comes back filled with the stories of the problems of the East Zone churches. Under Russian control, church participation is discouraged, party membership rewarded. The young person who joins a church often finds himself unable to enroll for higher education, use youth camping and hosteling facilities, apprentice for better jobs. The height of the conflict came several years ago when the Communists required all young people to take the Jugend Weihe or "youth dedication" oath, setting the date deliberately to conflict with the date of confirmation for the Lutheran Church. The Lutheran bishops, on their side, forbade their confirmands to take the Jugend Weihe. And the battle was on.

Many Americans have the impression that the Jugend Weihe is an oath of recent origin, formulated by the Communists. Martin Niemoeller gives the background of the entire conflict this way:

"The origin came with the attitude of the Christian Church opposing cremation. In 1890–1900 cremation came into vogue, and crematories were erected. Churches forbade pastors to partake of such ceremonies. Atheists and free thinkers arranged their own ceremonies to be used.

"After devising a ceremony for death, they said, 'Young

people in churches have confirmation. We should have a ceremony for the young, too.' So the Jugend Weihe—youth dedication—oath was invented. For children there was the Kinder Weihe, the substitute for baptism.

"There is no Jugend Weihe in Russia, Hungary, Poland. It is strictly a German custom, in East Germany and West Germany as well. The Communists made it one of their favored propaganda tricks. And the church fell into their trap.

"The church took up the cudgels—the German expression is 'took up the gloves'—and I was doubtful of the outcome from the start. It's good to fight for the gospel but confirmation is not the gospel. It is a custom with a church background. How important is it, unless people take advantage of it afterward? After confirmation, our people have the opportunity to partake of the Lord's table and go to church, but only 5 per cent of the confirmed people make use of these rights. It's a social duty and has nothing to do with Christianity.

"The question is, 'How much will you pay to retain a custom?' and not 'How much will you pay for your faith?' How many will stay with confirmation if in retaliation by the Communists—as is happening—they are not allowed to go to high school? They'll say, 'We'll take to the other social custom.'

"This fight had to end with defeat and it has ended with defeat.

"Everyone knows that confirmation is nothing on which you can build a structure which is to withstand a storm.

"It is a fight with a wooden sword against a poison sword."

26.

VISIT TO MOSCOW

How do you know that's true about Russia?" Martin Niemoeller was heckled during a speech he was making in East Berlin in 1951. "You've never been there."

"No, he retorted to the heckler, obviously a Communist. "You don't permit us to visit."

"If you were invited, would you come?" a Russian church official asked him in all seriousness later.

"If I were invited," he pledged, "I would come."

He was surprised and pleased later in the year to receive a formal invitation from the Patriarch Alexius of the Russian Orthodox Church. At last he had the opportunity to do something positive toward making his dream come true of the bridge between East and West.

He reported to the World Council of Churches and to Bishop Dibelius that he was accepting and would take all responsibility. Scarcely had he announced his plans when an avalanche of abuse descended on him. He was a tool of the Soviet, critics said. He was being politically irresponsible. He underestimated the Russian threat against the West and against world peace. The Kremlin had only invited him for reasons of propaganda and he had fallen into their trap.

Chancellor Adenauer said that "it was highly regrettable that a German of the stature of Dr. Niemoeller should stab his government in the back at this particular time." Niemoeller commented later it was as if "the mere attempt to take the pulse of the USSR were a crime against humanity."

After the trip Niemoeller wrote for *The Christian Century* in an endeavor to explain why he took the trip:

The constant complaint is that the chief hindrance to a peaceful understanding is lack of mutual trust. How, then, can anyone take it on himself to discredit in advance every little step that might help to create trust? Should not such attempts be given their chance, small though that may be?

I considered it my Christian duty to let the people in Moscow know that I am convinced not only that the West European peoples do not want a third world war but that there isn't a millionaire in America who would hesitate to sacrifice his entire fortune if he could thus prevent this catastrophe. . . . I likewise shall not refrain from telling Americans that, short as my stay in Moscow was, I got the impression that no one there wants a third world war either.

Some may smile at that and shrug their shoulders. For my part, as a Christian and a human being, I shall not leave undone what little I can do to encourage the mighty of the world to make ever-new efforts toward understanding. What is at stake is millions of human lives and human destinies, and no Christian may say of that, What concern is it of mine?

Niemoeller had three things in mind in planning the trip to Moscow. The first was the bridge of friendship. The second was an inquiry into church life in Russia and its fortunes under communism. The third was a practical hope that he might be able to do something to effect the release of German prisoners of war still being held by the Russians.

When his daughter, Hertha, then twenty-four years old, heard that he was going, she reminded him of a promise.

"You promised me if ever you went to Russia, I could accompany you. I studied Russian at the University of Frankfurt so I could be of use to you."

He asked for permission for Hertha to accompany him and it was granted.

The time span of the trip was brief, January 2–9, 1952. They traveled by plane and were met at the Moscow airport by correspondent Eddy Gilmore. Among the things they crowded into their visit were talks with the Patriarch Alexius on the possibility of closer relations between Eastern and Western churches, a call on East German Ambassador to Moscow Rudolf Apfelt, and Ivan Karpov, chief liaison official between the Russian Orthodox Church and the Soviet government. Niemoeller presented a plea to the Soviet Council of Ministers for the release of German prisoners which was not especially successful. He was told that only war criminals were still being held, not war prisoners, and his request to stay on and serve as their chaplain was refused.

He later said that his few days in Moscow seemed longer than his eight years in concentration camp but that the stay confirmed his belief that the Communists had not filled the Russian souls with marxist teachings. The Russian church was not a "dying church." Religion still had its place.

He observed and reported that there were sixty Orthodox churches in Moscow whereas in 1921 there was not a church left, and that the Baptist Church had 3,200,000 members.

"I was surprised to find Russian priests, alive, in good health and good financial condition," he said. "My first impression was of how badly we had been informed about them."

The most impressive phase of his trip was his participation in two Russian Christmas church services. Christmas is celebrated in Russia on January 7. The night before, Martin Niemoeller preached to a fervent and enthusiastic crowd of 2,500 in the Moscow Evangelical Baptist-Christian church. Jacob Zhidkov, head of the Russian Baptists, welcomed him, and Niemoeller preached in German, which was translated into Russian.

He brought greetings from German Baptist leader Paul Schmidt and from other German Baptists and German Lutherans. He spoke on the significance of the birth of Christ which "binds us together." He told of his years in concentration camp and the strength he had received from his Bible. His audience was visibly moved. The pine boughs and lights, the words "God Is Love" over the altar, and the spirit of peace on earth made a memorable scene. At midnight Niemoeller went to the Yelokhovskaya Sobor, Russian Orthodox Cathedral, and there presided with the patriarch behind the Icon of Stars. His impression in both services was that "here was a real Christian congregation and Christian priests . . . they know that Christ is their Lord and not Stalin."

Niemoeller was not deceived into believing the church a privileged institution in Russia, and he observed the sneering looks given by many to the priests as they walked down the street. He knew that the church is merely tolerated. But he was convinced that it was alive.

And he told United States churchmen through *The Christian Century:*

We cannot repudiate this church nor even declare ourselves indifferent to it. We shall have to think of it, pray for it, speak with it, and cleave to it, according to the word of the apostle: "And whether one member suffereth, all the members suffer with it; or if one member is honored, all the members rejoice with it." [I Corinthians 12:26.] For in such communion God desires to bless the community of Jesus Christ and through it all the generations on earth.

This was the message that Martin Niemoeller brought back from Russia. Far from being "taken in" by Russia, he had his daughter, Hertha, translate numerous sermons to see whether Russian priests were compromising Christian teaching with communist ideas, as German pastors had compromised with Nazi ideas. He found no such evidence, and it was a happy discovery for him.

In a University of Chicago Round Table discussion on February 24, 1952, in which Niemoeller participated with Miltan Mayer and Professor Wilhelm Pauck, he was asked if he felt the Western world could "do business with Stalin." The question, he replied, was not, "Can we do business with Stalin?" because the only alternative to "doing business" was to go to war, and in his opinion, war would mean the end of civilization. Therefore, the question should be, "How can we do business with Stalin? How can we live in a peaceful way— a more or less peaceful way—with Stalin?"

His conclusion was that "the responsibility of this situation rests with the so-called Christian world. We have to find a peaceful way not to lose the initiative to the world revolution of the Eastern world. We must gain the initiative for this peaceful competition on our side of the Western world in a wall of hearts that will not surrender to this Eastern ideology and in a wall of social endeavors that will compete in a peaceful way against anything which might call for a revolution."

This was Martin Niemoeller's message—that Christians must work together for peace, whether they live in Russia or in the Western world. He was not an advocate of communism; one can search his utterances in vain to find a single word in praise of the communist system of government. Indeed he found the Eastern world a strange one and a difficult one for the Westerner to comprehend. Being Martin Niemoeller, he loved many of the people and was impressed by them.

"After I returned home," he said, "I began to put things together and build a picture. Things stood out which had not been important at the time. For instance, I remembered a white-bearded taxi driver in front of the new University of Moscow under construction. Hertha spoke to him and he was proud of this achievement, this palace being constructed. He

said, 'Here on this spot, on these spacious hills on the high
bank of the river, here the caravans of punished people were
assembled and the barges went down the Volga and from
there to Siberia, and here on this very spot is now the university. And do you know who the first students will be who
will study here? The boys at the cranes, the people who built
the university. They will study here.' And he beamed."

Hertha remembers losing her temper one day when she felt
that they were being answered with nothing but propaganda
phrases at a meeting of communist students. She tried to tell
them that they didn't know what was going on in the world,
that they were being misled. Later her father said to her, "It's
no use getting angry and losing your temper because we want
to get to the people we are meeting, and if we lose our tempers
we have no possibility of getting to them." Now she thinks he
was right. "But at that age," she admitted, "you do not think
that compromise is the bigger part of life."

The tolerance that Martin Niemoeller tried to teach his
daughter, the Christian fellowship he tried to preach, were
misinterpreted by many of his fellow Germans. On January 14,
1952, his sixtieth birthday, Dr. Visser t'Hooft of the World
Council of Churches congratulated him in these words:

"He has shown by giving his whole life to it what it means
to live by one's beliefs in the midst of this world. . . . On this
day of celebration, therefore it should be very definitely stated
that his many friends in the World Council, including those
who disagree with him on many points, thank the Lord of the
church for giving them a Martin Niemoeller."

But on that sixtieth birthday on Brentanostrasse in front
of his house crowds congregated, waving signs and placards
that said, "Bolshevist! Communist! Go back to Russia!"

Martin Niemoeller had no desire to go back to Russia. In
fact, he tells an amusing story about the plane trip back when
he awakened from a brief nap to find the plane returning to

Moscow instead of going on to Berlin. For a moment he thought he was going to be apprehended for something he had said or done. Actually it was a weather problem that delayed the trip and they made a second start and the journey was uneventful.

He has taken occasion to go to other Iron Curtain countries, however. On June 13–16, 1953, he accepted an invitation from the World Peace Council and went to Budapest, where he met Bishop Berezky of the Reformed Church, returning to Berlin just in time to get into the June 17 riots of East Berlin. He returned to Hungary again on November 17, 1953, for the synod session of the church.

On this second trip Mrs. Niemoeller accompanied him. They flew from Vienna to Budapest with some complications, for when the time came to get on the plane they discovered they did not have their passports. The hotel clerk, as sometimes happens, had taken them the night before and had not returned them. It took quick action on the part of the home ministry to get permission for them to go on without their passports.

Niemoeller's impressions of Hungary were more positive than those of Russia. He found the western European atmosphere more familiar than the eastern attitudes of Russia. He felt that they had more in common.

"Russia is like visiting a strange country, like going to India, to the Far East," he said later. "In Russia one has the feeling that everything is alien, remote, a culture derived from Constantinople. In Hungary, Czechoslovakia, Poland, one senses that the culture was derived, like ours, from the Roman Empire."

He acquired great respect and affection for Bishop Berezky, a man whom he described as having "a tremendous load on his soul, with the necessity for getting along with the state." He was impressed by church attendance among Christians in Hungary, 20 per cent attendance instead of the weak 4 to 5 per cent in West Germany.

"Sometimes," he said, in one of those familiar acid outbursts, "I think if you are looking for good Christians, you should look not on this side of the Iron Curtain but on the other."

A trip that made a tremendous impression on both Niemoellers was one to India made in the winter of 1952–53. The annual meeting of the Central Committee of the World Council of Churches took place in Lucknow in the north of India December 29 through January 9. In addition Niemoeller had been asked to give one of the keynote lectures at the third World Conference of Christian Youth that met December 9–24 in Kottayam in the state of Travancore in the southern part of the country. He also was invited by the Indian government to participate in a ten-day Gandhi seminar, in New Delhi. The visit, long and varied, permitted some extensive impressions.

Their first impression was gained the night of their arrival. They flew from Cairo to Bombay, arriving so tired they had no intention of even looking at Bombay as they were driven to their hotel. But as they rode along, they observed that "on sidewalks and lawns, on each free spot with the exception of the road itself, we saw people sleeping—hundreds, thousands, tens of thousands—wrapped in a cotton cloth, their sole possession which was their robe of the day. Refugees from Pakistan. . . . In spite of our weariness we could not close one eye that night."

In the youth conference in Kottayam Niemoeller received the impression that communism was playing a big part, especially among the younger generation, but that "these young Communists are less concerned with the goal of world revolution than with the question of how to provide bread for a constantly growing population." Hatred for capitalism did not

seem important, he noted. The goal seemed to be easier working conditions.

He noted, too, a contrast between the Indians and the other
Asiatic representatives at the youth conference. The Indians—
"thanks to the wise politics of Great Britain," he pointed out—
had gained independence without violence. The other Asiatics
felt that their chance for liberty depended on their close connection with the Russian-Chinese world.

The Niemoellers met with Nehru and Mme. Pandit; Niemoeller and Nehru exchanged prison experiences.

But the most lasting impression of the trip came from the
Gandhi seminar. They were told that Gandhi had once said,
"When I am weary I can hear myself sing, 'Rock of ages, cleft
for me, let me hide myself in Thee.'" And they were struck
by many other sympathetic similarities between Gandhi's beliefs and those of Christianity.

Gandhi was influenced by the New Testament and the Sermon
on the Mount [Niemoeller wrote later], but he accepted only
from the New Testament that which can be found in the sacred
writings of Hinduism, of Vedanta and Bhagavad-Gita, and
basically he remained a Hindu. The Hindu "believes" in God
but does not believe that God reveals Himself. One has to seek
Him and while seeking one comes close to Him, some more,
some less, but the whole truth of God does not reveal Himself to us.

But when Gandhi preached non-violence, he was really preaching, Be not overcome of evil but overcome evil with good. The
Hindu has all of Christianity with the exception of Christ himself.

This and other trips were making Martin Niemoeller more
and more an ecumenical man of God. Those who term him a
tool of the Communists are much mistaken.

"The threat of bolshevism is a hundred times more dangerous than that of nazism," he said upon his return from Russia.
"I would a thousand times rather live on this side of the Iron

Curtain than the other. There, people are being stripped piece by piece of all that makes human living worth while."

At the same time he cannot see conflict with Russia.

"We Germans belong to the West, there is no doubt," he told correspondent Hanns Neuerbourg, "but on the other side of us is this uncanny colossus, this Russia, with whom we must live peacefully. We must find a *modus vivendi*."

And the only way Martin Niemoeller sees is that the bridge be built between East and West, the bridge described in the hymn, "In Christ there is no East and West. . . ."

27.

ANOTHER STORM ARISES

"MARTIN NIEMOELLER seems fated to live out his days as the center of controversy," commented *The Christian Century* on June 8, 1955.

A new storm had arisen, not over rearmament alone, or reunification, or Russia, but over his opinions on all three as well as that intangible but potent lack of understanding between Niemoeller and the conservative bloc in the Lutheran Church. The conflicts, the feuding, the internecine warfare were complicated subjects, said Martin Niemoeller, about which he could have "written several volumes, titling them, 'Persecution by the Church Following the Persecution of the Church.' "

Niemoeller was increasingly outspoken about the Bonn government and its policies. He had become increasingly friendly to the East. The General Synod of the United Evangelical Lutheran Church in Germany criticized his conduct of the "Kirchliches Aussenamt," the foreign office, and as a result he wrote to Bishop Dibelius that he would not perform the duties of his office until the criticism had been withdrawn.

Some of his activities that were criticized included an East Zone tour in late 1953 in which he praised the work of the Communist World Peace Council, and another Iron Curtain visit, this time to Prague, as the guest of Professor Joseph L. Hromadka of the Comenius Theological Seminary, a trip he took in April, 1954.

In August, 1954, he attended the World Council of Churches' meeting in Evanston, Illinois, and there he fought for stronge peace statements in the conclusions reached at various meetings. As for the situation in Germany, he said the primary problem was to make Christians out of church members.

"No state can destroy the church," he said, "but neither can any world power save the church. If it dies, it dies by suicide. Where it lives, it lives only by faith."

His attacks on Bonn began to be tinged with more and more criticism of Adenauer and the Catholic make-up of his government, with its preponderance, a near monopoly, in fact, of men of his own faith in policy-making positions. If division continued, he predicted, the Protestant church in Germany would be "ground between Roman Catholicism in the West and communism in the East."

"In western Germany," he added, "Protestants are confronted with a totalitarian Christianity even after the ghost of totalitarian race faith has been blown away."

In January, 1955, a circular signed by twenty-seven persons was distributed to deputies in the Bundestag before the first reading on the Paris treaties. Among the signers were Niemoeller of Hesse-Nassau, Dr. Heinrich Held of the Rhineland, Dr. Hans Stempel of the Palatinate, Dr. Ernst Wilm of Westphalia, Dr. Helmut Gollwitzer of Bonn, and theological officials from Mainz, Duesseldorf, Dortmund, West Berlin, Wuppertal, Heidelberg, Tuebingen, and Goettingen. The signers viewed with "deep concern" the Bundestag's prospective approval of rearmament and warned that passage of the treaties could "deeply shake our state and could endanger our all-German existence." It expressed the fear that the new army might mean new militarism, and would make reunification impossible, all of which Niemoeller had been saying.

It was also what the Social Democratic party, campaigning against Adenauer's C.D.U. party, had been saying. But it was not entirely the view of all the Protestants. At the synod meeting in March there was sharp disagreement. It ended with the synod voting out of office its president, Gustav Heinemann, an associate of Niemoeller who joined him in opposing rearmament and had appeared in a demonstration against rearmament at Frankfurt's St. Paul's Church.

There followed the meeting in Weimar of the VELKD, the United Evangelical Lutheran Church, conservative Lutheran branch of the EKID, and their call for reorganization of the EKID foreign office for the sake of Lutheran parishes abroad and to secure the confidence of all EKID groups in its foreign office. Niemoeller's reaction was to write to Bishop Dibelius submitting his resignation unless the charges were withdrawn.

As in most Niemoeller disputes there was more to the controversy than appeared on the surface. It was not entirely a fight between those who believed in arming Germany and those who believed in disarming and a cessation of atomic testing. Among the Lutheran groups there has always been a distrust of EKID for its tendency to become a "super church." They have maintained that the doctrinal and theological differences present in the Lutheran, the Reformed, and the United groups make it impossible for the three of them to form a church. EKID to the Lutherans was a federation, not a church. To the liberals, the Confessing churchmen, it was a church recognizing divisions within it.

The contention of the Lutherans was that EKID had no spiritual powers and so the foreign office could not play the part laid down for it as far as Lutherans in other lands are concerned. Many Lutherans in other lands do not agree with this way of thinking but align themselves with the Evangelical forces in Germany rather than the Lutheran.

"The Lutherans would like to bring about the German denominationalism of the nineteenth century," sighed one leading churchman, a friend and partisan of Niemoeller. "It was his opposition to denominationalism, his insistence that we have unity, that led to his difficulties in the foreign office. The foreign office was proof that German congregations abroad were united. It was the stronghold of a unifying element.

"There were all sorts of minor incidents leading to the flare-up. In Italy a Protestant church needed help. The Lutheran World Federation gave its members $5,000 and they became Lutherans. This is the sort of thing Niemoeller hates —financial pressure influencing a matter of conscience.

"Then there is the old-time Lutheran tradition of loyalty to state. Since he was opposed to rearmament, he was being disloyal to his government. They wanted a man who would be more acceptable to Bonn."

Then, lastly, there was personal bitterness of long standing between Niemoeller and Dr. Volkmar Herntrich, bishop of Hamburg. It was he, at the Weimar convention, who declared that the foreign office "does not direct its pastoral, spiritual, and organizational service as must be requested from it." And it was his remarks that Niemoeller termed "unworthy of an Evangelical theologian and intolerable within the Evangelical Church's sphere."

The threat of resignation was more than a threat. Niemoeller, Heinemann, and those opposing rearmament were in the minority. Niemoeller was relieved of his office.

Protested *The Christian Century* in its June, 1955, commentary:

Some of the charges made against them have been as wild and as unfounded as those leveled against Americans accused of playing the communist game. Men like Niemoeller and Heinemann simply do not trust a rearmed Germany. As one follows the press reports of Hitler generals flocking back to take a hand in the Bonn rearmament, who can be sure they are wrong?

In the fall of 1955 Niemoeller visited the United States again, but this time his visit was under new sponsorship, that of the Fellowship of Reconciliation, an organization of religious pacifists.

While Niemoeller had been turning more and more toward preaching peace, this was the first time he had spoken under pacifistic auspices. The tone of his addresses on this visit was set in New York where he urged Christians to "wake up and realize that war is contrary to the will of God," and that pacifism is offering humanity its "last chance."

He predicted that Germany would be reunited in five years. If reunification did not come about through cooperation between the West and the East, he said, it was highly probable that some strong militaristic leader would arise and join the armies of both halves to create an ardently militaristic state. Psychologically, Germany was longing for reunification, he said. The people would be as ready for a military leader under the new setup as they had been ready for Hitler.

His talks on this visit also reflect strongly the effects of his visit to the Gandhi conference and his interest in the Far East. In Nashville, Tennessee, he declared that the job of the Christian church in the world today is to make peace. Taking his text from Luke 16:8, the parable of the unjust steward, he accused the Christian nations of being unjust stewards of God's world.

"For the past three hundred years," he said, "the world has been under the domination of Christian nations, and today more than half of the world does not have enough to eat. The feeling of race superiority exists among the Christian nations; the cold war and its resulting armament race continues.

"The Western nations are seeking peace, but without consideration of China or India, who together have nearly one half the world's population. Such a peace is impossible. I predict that in one hundred years the supremacy of the white man will be gone. Two thirds of the people in this world are colored; in one hundred years these people will either be dominating the rest of the world or will be working as equals with the rest of the world. Which it will be depends upon the way Christian nations act in the next few years."

The year 1956 in the German Protestant world was devoted primarily to the planning and execution of the sixth *Kirchentag* celebration. The *Kirchentag*—literally "Church Day"—is a week-long program culminating in a gigantic mass rally of hundreds of thousands of Protestants who come from all over Germany, East and West, and from all corners of the globe.

Dr. Franklin H. Littell, chairman of the Ecumenical Committee for the 1956 *Kirchentag,* has called it "a most significant development in the postwar life of the church because it is forward looking. It is not afraid to use mass rallies because the method has been exploited by political demagogues. It perceives that the isolated individual needs fellowship in solidarity. Hence it transforms that mass expression of solidarity into a public demonstration of Christian witness."

The first *Kirchentag,* brought to life by Dr. Reinold von Thadden-Trieglaff, met in Essen in 1950, Berlin in 1951, Stuttgart in 1952, Hamburg in 1953, and—most significantly —in Leipzig in the East Zone in 1954. Because the event was becoming so tremendous in size, it was decided to let two years elapse before the next one, which was held in 1956, August 8–12, in Frankfurt, the largest city of the church state headed by church president Martin Niemoeller.

The theme chosen was a noble one: Be ye reconciled with God.

The tone was set in the opening service in the Roemerplatz at which Niemoeller preached on the theme itself. Some 60,000 persons jammed the streets of the square. The pulpit was built on the second floor of a partially bombed church, visible to the crowds. Banners decorated the square.

In Niemoeller's sermon there was not a breath of his opinion on earthly reunification. Instead, he preached the reunification offered by God which, once accepted, becomes the direction of man's daily life. In part he said:

"God holds out His Hand and He is waiting for us to take it. No, God does not wait; God seizes our hand and He does not withdraw His hand even though we want to push it back. He does not even withdraw it when we crucify it. At all costs He wants to make us take the hand which He holds out for us. It is high time, very high time, that we do so, and let go everything else to which we cling: the fear which turns our life into hell, the sorrow which is a heavy burden for us, the hostility. . . . The reconciliation to God as a gift of God in Jesus Christ is our daily task in our life in the community in this world, no empty promises for an uncertain future, but a task today and here. For God wants 'that all men shall be saved and come to a knowledge of truth.' Reconciliation is not a Utopian scheme; it is the reality of the grace of God."

It was a strong plea for the building of bridges, not only the bridge between East and West but the bridge of brotherhood around the world.

There was a jarring note in the Christian fellowship of the 1956 *Kirchentag*. On August 9, the second day, at the big public reception in the Rathaus, Martin Niemoeller's name was omitted from the list of speakers. Quite obviously he was snubbed because the political leaders present felt he might say things unpopular with the government. In understandable anger, but with a pique many do not understand, Martin Niemoeller strode out of the meeting.

The Rev. Dr. O. Walter Wagner, executive secretary of the Metropolitan Church Federation of Greater St. Louis, who was present when the snub occurred, quoted in his report on

Kirchentag, Niemoeller's analysis of the state of affairs in East and West Germany.

Said Niemoeller: "The East Zone has a Russianized army. The West Zone has an Americanized army. Both armies are totally unwanted by the German people. This is the soil for a new nationalism. Someday, and that soon, some new leader—Fuehrer—will play both ends against the middle. 'Are we not Germans?' will be the new Fuehrer's slogan. 'What kind of business is this—Russians leading us in the East, Americans in the West? Isn't it time that we assert our German rights?' "

Continued Dr. Wagner, "Martin Niemoeller feels deeply that such a nationalism would be dangerous. He advocates a neutrality like that of Switzerland and feels the present division will never bring reunification.

"The opposition party, the minority party at present, has already declared that in the next national elections their main platforms will be to rescind rearmament. One can understand why the present political party would like to silence men like Niemoeller."

Later that year, on November 4, 1956, Dr. Wagner had occasion to introduce Niemoeller as he spoke for a Reformation Day program in Kiel Auditorium in St. Louis. Said Dr. Wagner:

"When our generation is seen in the perspective of history three men will emerge as makers of our history and they will not be Hitler, Stalin, or Mussolini. Kagawa will have conditioned the affairs of the Far East; Gandhi of Asia; and Martin Niemoeller of middle Europe."

28.

NIEMOELLER AT HOME

OCCASIONALLY in a heated discussion on disarmament versus rearmament, pacifism versus nuclear testing, some sly person will say to Martin Niemoeller, "So you believe in non-violence. What would you do if some brute were to attack your wife?"

"I would kill him, of course," Niemoeller says, without batting an eye.

He finds no incongruity in his support of mass reconciliation over mass retaliation on the one hand, and his tigerlike protective attitude toward his wife and family on the other. Nor does he find any incongruity in his sharp attacks in the public and political arena and his warm tenderness at home.

Most men in the public eye have two personalities, a public and a private one. Martin Niemoeller's merge to some extent. Many meeting him in the most public of places have basked in the radiance of his warm smile. Many who have seen him in intimate situations have observed that he can get as annoyed when he is kept waiting for a cup of coffee as when he is made to cool his heels by a British admitting officer.

But while many people have been angered by his public actions and utterances, no one could meet Martin Niemoeller and visit in the comfortable circle of his home without a feeling of admiration and fondness no matter how he might have felt before.

The first thing that impresses most visitors is the love between Martin and Else Niemoeller. Rarely does one see such
frank, unashamed devotion and dependence between two
people past the honeymoon stage.

Else Niemoeller worships her husband, flies to his defense
in conflict and criticism. This adulation he accepts. But the
moment she is out of sight he searches the crowd for her. Where
has "Mutti" gone?

"Mutti, what shall I wear? Mutti, what shall I tell the
people? Mutti, give me a text for the sermon."

He loves to tease his wife, and his favorite jokes are about
henpecked husbands and bossy wives. There is the one about
the husband and wife arguing in a canoe over whether a knife
or scissors was the better cutting agent. He maintained knife,
she scissors, and they argued so violently they upset their
canoe and drowned. But in the instant before the husband
went under, he saw his wife's arm still above water, her fingers
still cutting in a scissors motion.

"There are two kinds of marriages," he quips, "those in
which the wife prevails and the unhappy ones."

Else Niemoeller smiles tolerantly. She does not mind being
his straight man. She knows her conversational reflexes are
not so rapier sharp and cutting as his. She knows her turn of
mind is more sober.

And yet it is he who often turns to her for sound advice, for
the worldy wisdom he does not possess.

"Surely," he said to her on one occasion, "after what I
have done there is no one who would wish to harm me?"

Mutti shook her head.

"Oh, Martin, Martin, you are so naïve."

Perhaps they can be best characterized by saying Martin
Niemoeller is brilliant, and Else Niemoeller is wise.

At the dinner table Martin and Else sit on a bench close together, separated only by the dachshunds who nose their sleek,

pointed heads onto the pastor's lap for a taste of food. There are two dachshunds now. Ratz was given to them when they lived in the castle in Buedingen, by a friend, Margaret Jahn. He is twelve years old but has the delusion that he is a puppy. Freschdachs, two years old, came from a church official in Darmstadt. He was hit by a motorcycle two years ago and almost died. As he regained consciousness, they carried him to the dinner table and he begged for a piece of bread. They decided he was going to live.

The dachshunds are very much a part of the family. Fräulein Dora had their pictures made for the pastor's sixtieth birthday.

Fräulein Dora, after all these years, is very much a part of the family, too, often speaking up as frankly as if she were one of the children. Her nephew, Hans Schmidt, a young man in his twenties, lives with them now, and young Martin, who has just graduated from law school, is often at home.

When Tini is at home, his father sometimes has difficulty finding his own clothing. Suits, shoes, pajamas are missing. He is about to start on a trip and looks for his raincoat. Tini has it.

"A surprise for Father," says Pastor Niemoeller grimly. Then he laughs. "Well, this is practical Christian communism. Nobody in this house has a feeling that anything in the house doesn't belong to all."

He himself is casual about his possessions and he says they can disappear for all he cares.

"Except old papers," he specifies. "I was meant by predestination to be an old-paper collection man."

The other children are not home as often as the youngest. Brigitte has come to the United States to work, and Hermann, who came to the United States in 1952, is a doctor at Yale. Hermann had intended coming here just for a visit but liked it and stayed on; now he feels a sense of confinement when he is in Germany surrounded only by German people.

Hermann argues with his father over many things—who started the Korean war, for instance—but basically they agree. When someone attacks his father's conciliatory attitude toward the Russians with the argument that the Russians do not value human life, Hermann cites his wartime experience. They were attacking a town in Silesia, the Germans in open fields, the Russians inside houses. Two men started carrying a wounded man away and everyone expected them to be mowed down, obvious targets. But all firing ceased until they were gone. Hermann has felt better about the Russians because of that simple humanitarian act. He feels, from experience, too, that "armed conflict serves no useful purpose."

Brigitte thinks that she is more pacifistic than her father ever could be. She agrees with him in every way and thinks he is "one of the last real prophets of political thinking." She regrets that he has not gotten along better with journalists and thinks much of the misunderstanding has come from misconstrued interviews.

"Many people say he is wrong. He is too far from reality," says Brigitte. "But as long as I can remember people have been saying he was wrong, and it has turned out that he was right."

Hertha, the other daughter, is at home only occasionally. She is married to Wilhelm von Klewitz, diplomat and member of an old Silesian family. There was a family turmoil when they were married; the Niemoellers wanted them to wait awhile and for a long time there was coolness. Then with the grandchildren things smoothed over a little. Brigitte and Hermann have much of their mother's diplomacy, coupled, in Hermann's case, with his father's smile, a resemblance that is startling. Hertha is much more likely to "blow off the handle," as does her father.

Hertha and her husband and children moved from Afghanistan to the Philippines in 1958, and the mother and children spent the summer in Wiesbaden. Her children are Martin, then five, Ulrika, two, and the baby, Anna Christine. Martin Niemoeller's children call him "Vati." His grandchildren call him and his wife Opa and Oma.

The other son, Jan, a lawyer, is also married and lives across from the castle at Buedingen. He and his wife, Irene, have a baby. Jan is perhaps the most outgoing of all the children, combining his father's charm and his mother's diplomacy.

But the Niemoellers play no apparent favors among their children, and the family portraits are hung indiscriminately on all the walls. In the living room and dining rooms are pastels of young Martin as a baby in 1936, and of Hermann, a painting of Jochen, blown-up snapshots of Hertha and Jutta at the beach, a pencil sketch of Hermann at the piano, pictures of Jan, of Brigitte.

The walls are well decorated at 3 Brentanostrasse. In the hall is a Rembrandt, a gift from Dietrich Bonhoeffer. Across from it is a framed verse in Latin, a Middle Ages hymn, that goes:

> *Fac ut possim demonstrare*
> *quam sit dulce te amare*
> *tecum pati—tecum flere*
> *tecum semper congaudere.*
> *Amen*

Martin Niemoeller translates it as "Make it so that I can show how sweet it is to love Thee, to suffer for Thee, to cry with Thee, and to praise Thee always. Amen."

In a small parlor just off the hall is some of the furniture, birchwood with black and gold trim, which they had in the house at Dahlem. The living room is comfortably but not ostentatiously furnished. The record player in the corner is much used, whether Hans is playing his Louis Armstrong records of American jazz, or Martin Niemoeller suddenly decides he must hear the recording Tini made one night of a nightingale outside their window. The Niemoellers are a musical family and many a delighted American guest has spent an evening singing in their home. The exterior of their home is of less interest to them but there is a rose garden, a sandbox for children, and a yardful of chickens.

The pastor's brother Wilhelm emphasizes that his brother is not a businessman and has never bothered trying to amass a fortune but lives on his salary. Money is of no consequence to him.

This does not mean that he is careless, however. He can be very generous but he does not waste money. Mrs. Niemoeller still remembers that when she was a young married woman, he would say to her, "You must buy your *broetchen* from money you have, not from money you are going to have."

Niemoeller manages his time in the same methodical way in which he manages his money and leads an incredibly busy life. Each morning he is up at five or six. Fräulein Dora brings his pot of coffee into the dining room, and frequently he answers letters or gets an early start on work. At eight o'clock his chauffeur, Werner Berghauser, picks him up in the black Mercedes, and they start for Darmstadt and his church office, a forty-kilometer, forty-five-minute drive.

Niemoller has been the president of the Evangelical Church in Hesse and Nassau since 1947. He was a candidate for the office of church president and elections were coming up in both Westphalia and Hesse-Nassau. He decided he would accept whichever one came first. The Hesse-Nassau preceded the other by two days. He thinks now it is just as well that he didn't go back to his Westphalian home because there would have been too many old friends there. However, in Germany, where the language has such definite dialect distinctions, it is difficult to live in a place where "as soon as you open your mouth, people know you're a foreigner." In Hesse-Nassau they use the soft "cha," and you don't know "when they say *'Kirche'* if they're saying 'church' or 'cherry,' " says their church president.

There is a great deal of administrative work in his job, more than a bishop in America would have, he believes. All church work is centralized. He must approve the salary of every pastor in his district, confirm every budget of every local church, distribute the church tax. This work takes a staff of a hundred in Darmstadt.

Darmstadt, for centuries the residence of the grand duke of Hesse, has its landmark, a statue to Ludwig II—"The Long Ludwig"—a tall, red pillar in the square. The church office has recently moved to a bank building on Paulusplatz and is a busy place.

On Tuesday, visitors' day, for instance, the church president may hold a conference on home mission work, on pastor organization, may talk to a theologian, a lawyer, an architect, discuss the training of schoolteachers. Everything from the examinations for students to the signing of the certificate for parishioners celebrating an eightieth, ninetieth, or hundredth birthday comes before him.

His secretary, Ingeburg Hahnemann, who has been with him four years, scurries around, leaps to his side when he calls, takes his fast dictation.

This is only half of his work. The other half is done at home where a secretary works with him, answering voluminous foreign correspondence, planning the many trips to peace conferences, to other lands, cataloguing his church publications.

Each Sunday he preaches, sometimes at the Stadtkirche in Darmstadt, sometimes at the big Katharinenkirche in Frankfurt where 800 fill the church, sitting around the sides and back.

He starts writing his sermons on Saturday at 9 A.M. but makes all kinds of excuses to keep from getting down to work.

Usually he has finished one and a half or two pages by noon. He naps after lunch, the main meal of the day, and continues at four in the afternoon, working on through the evening at white heat, sometimes until one or two o'clock in the morning. He writes his sermons out in full, usually on a typewriter that has served him for many years.

He takes the whole manuscript with him into the pulpit but does not appear to refer to it. He is always a little nervous before he stands up to speak; the amount of nervous tension is in direct proportion to how much time he has to think about it. He likes to preach best when he feels he really has something to say, and especially likes to talk to large crowds. His wife says she can tell when they are responding to him; he seems to draw strength from the audience's response.

After a Sunday-morning sermon Niemoeller often goes into the country or the mountains, perhaps to nearby Odenwald to a small village church. Very often the town will be decorated with flags in his honor and he is always genuinely surprised, and usually tries to pass it off by pretending there must be a fete in the making.

He especially enjoys the small churches, the meeting with small groups, the gifts of cake and cookies they press on him to take home, the armfuls of flowers. After such a day he is happy, relaxed. On the way home with Herr Berghauser he will burst into song, "Oh what a beautiful morning". . ."They've got an awful lot of coffee in Brazil" ("I love that line—'they put coffee in the coffee in Brazil,' " he chuckles.) "With a little bit of luck . . . Get me to the church on time. . . ."

He is especially fond of the music from *My Fair Lady,* has seen it twice, and hopes to see it a third time. Mrs. Niemoeller enjoys it, too. Pointedly, she has told her husband she particularly appreciated the song, "Why Can't a Woman Be Like a Man?"

Martin Niemoeller leads a mechanized life, hurrying from

appointment to appointment in his car, and perhaps his chauffeur is the man who knows him best. Certainly bland, unperturbed, ruddy-faced Herr Berghauser is a man to deal with temperament.

"Hist, hist, whish, whish," Pastor Niemoeller urges him on when he feels he is lagging behind another car. Then he jokes over his back seat driving and tells another of his favorite stories—this one about the woman who nagged her husband until he went through a red light. Stopped by a policeman, the man sat patiently while the woman continued to nag him unmercifully, until the policeman interrupted with, "That your wife?" following it up with a sympathetic, "Go ahead, brother." When Martin Niemoeller feels he has given one too many "whishes," he is likely to sit back, laugh at himself, and say, "Go ahead, brother."

Conscientious and hard-working, Martin Niemoeller tries to keep up with all his thousand churches in addition to his other work, and has not taken a vacation in two years. When he does vacation, at some such spot as Interlaken, Switzerland, he does so vigorously, with a tour a day to some point of interest.

He likes sports. He perfected his game of ping-pong in concentration camp and still plays it when he can, and likes to swim when he has a chance.

He enjoys many relaxations such as reading, is interested in poetry which he wrote as a young man. He does not mind reading a novel if it is brief.

"I am one of those people who never can understand why they say something in ten thousand words when it can be said in one thousand," he once said.

The books in his study give some indication of his wide and varied interests. Among those he read in concentration camp are *Darkness at Noon, Microbe Hunters, Victoria Regina, The Unvanquished, Journeyman, Mill on the Floss, The Works of Oliver Goldsmith, Last of the Mohicans, Lady of the Lake,* and his favorite "Jalna" books of family life.

Also in this study are the numerous framed honorary degrees that Martin Niemoeller has received. In the study, as in the living room below, is a portrait of his kindly smiling father.

Martin Niemoeller himself is a fine-looking man, trim of figure, tan and healthy of face, energetic as he mounts the stairs two at a time with never a hint of the heart attacks he suffered at the end of the war, of the pallor and deep-etched lines during his concentration camp days. Sometimes he has an occasional twinge, he calls it a "cramp," in his heart. "It is nothing, it will pass." He brushes off sympathy as he takes a pill.

Fussy about his appearance, he gets cross if something is wrong with his clothes, and a missing button will drive him crazy. He has a preference for navy-blue suits and likes to wear a beret when he is taking a long car trip.

About once a year he goes to a movie, preferring funny ones to get his mind off things. But he would rather spend his evenings in good conversation, arguing points of law with his lawyer sons, discussing world affairs or theology.

Anyone is likely to drop in at the Niemoeller house. There are visitors from all over the world, and often they come to ask him questions.

One night a young man named Bill Fee, a friend of Hermann who had gotten acquainted with him first as a pen pal, stopped in. Young Fee is a government worker by profession, a churchman and Sunday-school teacher by avocation.

"What does it mean to you to be a Christian?" he had come to ask Niemoeller.

Martin Niemoeller gave the question the serious consideration he gives every question.

"To ask the man, this man whom we call Christ what He wants us to do, to accept His leadership and His decision on how to lead your life, how to lead my life. Ask it as Paul did on the road to Damascus. That is the real center of Christian life—what am I to do, how am I to live—the question, as St. Paul asked it, 'What wilt Thou, Oh Lord, have me to do?' "

It is usually too late when Martin Niemoeller gets to bed. His day, begun at 5 A.M., often ends after midnight. Once his wife noted the single entry in his diary, "*Muede—muede—muede*"—"Tired—tired—tired." But he sleeps instantly, the minute his head touches the pillow.

Over the bed is his navy Muetzenband, the silk ribbon embossed in gold from his navy hat. It is his tie to the Lippe River and childhood. Beside him is his beloved wife.

29.

THE HOPE FOR PEACE

A VERY wise man once said to me, 'Everyone has a time in his life when he is at his best.' For Martin Niemoeller, his time came when he opposed Hitler and nazism. After it was over, he refused to admit that he had had his time."

The speaker was a German, one of the many who do not think of Martin Niemoeller as a prophet but as a gadfly, buzzing around and annoying those in power.

His fellow countryman continued:

"He has made enemies in a typically German fashion, by always saying what is wrong but never what to do instead. Germans are good diagnosticians but not very good therapists. He can tell you exactly the weak spot, what is wrong, but when you ask him what to do instead, he becomes evasive."

Many in western Germany and the rest of the world would agree with that statement. But Niemoeller's admirers strongly disagree. Niemoeller has a positive program, they say. It is the same program that Christ preached, the Christian way.

Whereas in the earlier years Niemoeller's criticism of the German government concerned things specifically German, today his criticism is directed at the conduct of world affairs between East and West. Insisting that he is not an "organized pacifist," he is teaching and preaching peace.

"We can no longer debate the question whether war is good or bad, whether there is such a thing as a just war or an unjust war," he wrote in the magazine published by the Fellowship of Reconciliation, a pacifist organization.

"War—at least between powers that are able to build this bomb as their last resort—has ceased to be a means at all. War is no longer good or bad, just or unjust. However you look at it, war under these circumstances is madness. Madness cannot be characterized by 'good' or 'bad' or 'just' or 'unjust.' "

One of Niemoeller's criticisms of Western policy is that it has led western Germany along two diametrically opposed lines since the end of the war. From 1945 to 1948 the German people were re-educated along pacifistic lines. They were taught that to take up guns was against the will of God. Then early in 1950 their re-education took a different slant. The use of weapons was only bad for the wrong reasons, and the fight for the Western world was not the wrong reason. It became a Christian cause to be in favor of rearmament.

In the past several years there has been as much dissension in the Protestant church groups in Germany over rearmament, atomic warfare, and nuclear testing as there ever was over Hitler. In 1954, when the controversy was raging, Niemoeller, Bishop Dibelius, and Professor Gollwitzer arranged to talk with Germany's three leading nuclear physicists, Professor Otto Hahn, who split the atom in the Kaiser Wilhelm Institute in 1937; Professor Heisenberg; and Professor von Weizsaecker. In the course of this conversation Pastor Niemoeller put a question to Professor Hahn:

"What do you think Hitler would have done if he had had this bomb when at last he sat in the cellar of the Reich's chancellery in Berlin, and his fate had overtaken him and nothing was left but to surrender or to commit suicide?"

Professor Hahn smiled.

"In that case, my dear Pastor Niemoeller," he replied, "you and I would not be bothering our brains about it here and now."

Niemoeller does not believe that either the East or the West

—Russia or the United States—will exercise humanitarian control and refrain from using the bomb if the chips are down.

"Rather than accept what it regards as 'ultimate evil,' the dominance of another way of life," he has said, "the nation facing defeat will resort to the weapon that can obliterate all life. And that will mean the end of mankind on the surface of our planet!"

It was after his conversation with the physicists that Niemoeller formally joined the Fellowship of Reconciliation, through Professor Siegmund Schultze of Dortmund, giving as his reason, "We have to work for peace if we want to prevent war."

Criticized for attending meetings of the World Peace Council, a Russian-supported peace organization, Niemoeller replied:

"I am a Christian, not a Communist. I know that the World Peace Council is supported by Russian money, but I would rather the Russians spent their money on fostering the World Peace Council than on building tanks and bombers."

He has another rather sharp answer for those who ask if he does not consider the leaders of many peace movements Communists or leftist in sympathy.

"If this is the case, it is our fault," he has said. "It is a sad commentary on Christians, if peace actions are led in non-communist countries by Communists. They should be led by Christians."

For Americans who are leaders in the peace movement he has only praise.

Of Dr. Edwin T. Dahlberg: "If I wouldn't trust Dahlberg, I wouldn't trust my own wife." Of A. J. Muste of the Fellowship of Reconciliation: "I'm sure when I get to heaven I will see him there."

What should the Christian do in this fight? Robert Wuliger,

writing in *The Christian Century* on January 29, 1958, pointed out that one wide-spread misconception was that Pastor Niemoeller believes a Christian cannot accept military service.

"I, for one, cannot understand how someone who believes in Christ can take up arms," he has said. But he does not presume to force this interpretation on anyone else, and added, "If someone else thinks that it is compatible with the love of Christ to take up arms, that is his own affair.

"As I know Christ, I should do what He would do. I think that Christ would not bear arms but rather find ways to bring the love of God to His neighbors among whom are His enemies."

What should the Western world do to promote peace? On this point Niemoeller is vehement. Talk and more talk is the answer, he says, and then with some impatience, "I do not understand it when diplomats whose business it is to talk, refuse to talk. I like to talk because I feel I can get the better of an argument. I see nothing in open talk and discussion with Communists which I should fear. Either they are cranks and deceivers and I can unveil that deceit or they are really approachable which is what we all ought to hope for. Maybe things will not open up at first; then we might have to talk quite a while longer. But how shall we come to trust each other if we refuse to talk?"

Western policy was criticized by Niemoeller indirectly when he was asked recently if he thought Russia was intent on waging war.

"I was often asked that question ten years ago concerning Stalin's intentions," he said. "And I always said I tried to put myself in Stalin's shoes and ask what I would do. And I answered that if I were Stalin and I thought of having a war with the West I would not risk it as long as there was an even chance. Instead, I would go into the countries like China where the people are very poor and where I could win them over by raising their living standards. I would go into India, into black Africa, and make friends. Then, if I felt the West had to be destroyed, I would wait until the odds were more in my favor, say a risk of eight to one.

"This is just what Russia has done. She has made friends in the less fortunate countries. And it is what the West is not doing."

Looking to the future, there is one element that may influence the conflict between East and West, Niemoeller surmises, and that is the conflict between the white and colored races.

"Sometimes I feel that the East-West problem never will be solved," he has said, "but that the other will grow to such an extent that the East-West problem will not disappear but will become unimportant."

Meanwhile, Martin Niemoeller continues to work in a practical way at his ambition, to build the bridge between East and West, and to bring his views before the public. At the tenth meeting of the Central Committee of the World Council of Churches, held at the Yale Divinity School in New Haven, Connecticut, in August, 1957, he was instrumental in getting a strong statement on atomic tests and disarmament into the proceedings. Its last paragraph written by him read:

We are bound to ask whether any nation is justified in continuing the testing of nuclear weapons while the magnitude of the dangers is so little known and while effective means of protection against these dangers are lacking. We must ask further whether any nation is justified in deciding on its own responsibility to conduct such tests, when the people of other nations in all parts of the world who have not agreed may have to bear the consequences. Therefore we call upon each nation conducting tests to give full recognition to this moral responsibility as well as to considerations of national defense and international security.

In great demand as a speaker at peace conferences, Martin Niemoeller was featured on programs in Italy, Denmark, Sweden, and Germany during the summer of 1958. Most of these meetings attracted delegates from all the countries of the world including those behind the Iron Curtain. At a meeting in Bueckeburg, Germany, in August, 1958, these representatives sat down together: Evald Gunarsen, Denmark; Jean Goss, Austria; Professor Dr. Hannes de Graaf, Holland; Archbishop Gustav Turs, Latvia; Archbishop Jaan Kiivit, Estonia; Propst Andrej Rastoguew, Russia; the Rev. A. J. Muste, Professor Henry J. Cadbury, Herbert Hadley, and Milton Mayer, United States; the Rev. Leslie Hayman, New Zealand; Clarence Bauman, Canada; and from Germany, Praeses D. Ernst Wilm, Propst D. Heinrich Grueber, Oberkirchenrat Heinz Kloppenburg, Professor D. Hans Iwand, Dr. Wolfgang Schweitzer, Pastor R. Wilhelm Mensching, Studienrat Dr. Hans Gressel, and Niemoeller.

Pacifism is not only a subject for the public forum with Niemoeller these days. His views carry over into every casual contact and into the pulpit. As in Hitler's days, they are voiced with vigor.

On his 1958 visit to the United States, Pastor Niemoeller delivered his first two sermons in Philadelphia, Pennsylvania, one on Sunday morning, June 29, at the Church of the Holy Trinity on Rittenhouse Square, the second at an open-air meeting sponsored by the All Saints Episcopal Church at Rhawnhurst, a suburb, that night.

In the service at Holy Trinity he took as his text the verses from St. John concerning the anxiety of the high priests and Pharisees over the success of Jesus and His followers, ending with the sentence, "Then from that day forth they took counsel together for to put Him to death."

As in the days of Jesus, Pastor Niemoeller warned, the great dangers to the Christian Church do not come from without, from the unbelievers, but from those close to us. Jesus had become "politically suspect, a danger to the nation."

"He was teaching a different way of behavior from that of the enemy," Niemoeller said, "not to resist evil but to overcome evil with good. As long as He only talks, He may be considered just one more specimen among the queer idealists who are to be found in every generation. They arise, they talk, they disappear, and are forgotten. But when His teachings begin to show effect, they become dangerous.

"For centuries," he continued, "the church has not obeyed His rules but has tried to get around them. Just as Caiphus did, we ask how can we defend ourselves, how can we survive if we really try to learn to love our enemies and to overcome good with evil . . . The Romans—the Russians—will come and take away our nation."

God gave us two rules, Niemoeller said, "Thou shalt love the Lord thy God with all thy heart and with all thy soul and with all thy mind," and "Thou shalt love thy neighbor as thyself."

"We have put another commandment first," he said. "It is: We shall love ourselves. We call it the law of self-preservation—safety first, my safety first."

He then repeated a story he has often told about what he calls his "second conversion." It took place at Dachau where he often sat wondering how he would behave when they came to lead him to his death. Would he scream, "You murderers, you don't know what you're doing?" Or would he pray, "Father, forgive them." It was not until he neared the end of his imprisonment that an illuminating thought occurred to him—the thought that Christ had died for his hangman, for the black-uniformed man who guarded him. It was a moment he has never forgotten.

At Rhawnhurst he emphasized the same lesson, this time

taking as his text Matthew 10:16, "Behold I send you forth as sheep in the midst of the wolves: be ye therefore wise as serpents, and harmless as doves." And who were the wolves? Again, not the unbelievers, but "These highly religious people were the wolves that tore the sheep, the lamb of God," said Niemoeller.

"The Son of man must suffer many things. He must be rejected by the elders, chief priests, and scribes. He must be killed. But why? Because He is sent forth to abolish the ruling law of the wolves, the law of the jungle, the law of nature as we civilized people know it. The law invented by sinful man instead of the law we ought to obey—that man must love God and love his fellow man."

Martin Niemoeller's message was not always popular during the struggle against the Nazis. It is not always popular today. In the village church at Kreuth, Bavaria, just after the August, 1958, peace meeting at Bueckeburg, Pastor D. Hegl of Tegernsee barred him from the pulpit because he said, "Dr. Niemoeller has frequently labeled atomic-armaments promoters as atheists."

About the same time Niemoeller spoke in Cologne on "atom death," voicing the sentiment that Germany must be a bridge or a battlefield. After his talk he posed for a picture by one of Hiroshima, holding aloft the display torch. The torch set off a blaze of criticism and some hinted that Niemoeller would be called to account for his actions.

Perhaps most spectacular was his treatment in England in October, 1958, when he went there on a speaking tour, one of many he has made in that country. He had been cross-examined on occasions before but this time, as he wrote in an open letter to the church people and clergy of England, he was kept standing for fifty minutes as an official questioned him about his purpose in coming to England. Asked what he intended to preach, he replied tartly, "The gospel of Jesus Christ." This was not enough for the official, and there was more waiting, more delay.

By the time clearance had been granted, Niemoeller was in a fine state of agitation and had decided to return to Frankfurt and cancel his British tour.

The official's conduct was correct [he concluded his open letter], but my situation was completely insufferable.

Everybody stared at me as at one suspected of a theft or crime. I was not even offered a chair [as had been done on two former occasions]. I was hardly capable of controlling my excitement. After I had conferred with Pastor Walker by telephone and had written explanatory letters to the other places to which I had been invited I returned in the late afternoon, decided to cancel all my acceptances to England for 1959 and 1960, and to accept invitations only on conditon that there would be a formal assurance added that I would not be treated any worse than any other German citizen upon entering English soil.

In January, 1959, Niemoeller incurred trouble in his own country. At a rally of the Union for National Freedom in Kassel he condemned military training and made reference to commando training in World War II as a "high school for potential criminals." The West German government interpreted this as a slur at present military training and through Defense Minister Franz Josef Strauss brought legal action on a charge of criminally slandering the army.

These many brushes with authority have had their effect on Niemoeller's standing in his own church. At the March, 1958, elections he was re-elected to his post as church president of Hesse and Nassau by only one vote. Both the clerical and secular press commented that Niemoeller's foes had been surprised at the closeness of the election. Had he been defeated, who would have taken his place? Said the secular *Die Welt*:

Niemoeller has made friends and many enemies but he leaves nobody cold. He is fought about by the members in the church who would like to compete with him. But even his opponents admit that there is no applicant who could match his spiritual standing and who could match him in church historical importance and regard in the Christian world. . . . Among those who really know him on a theological basis are those who are united to him almost with a hate-love and hold him in esteem as a human being and a stirring preacher even though they are repelled by his reckless utterances to political questions.

And before the election the *Kirche in der Zeit* made a similarly penetrating analysis:

What Niemoeller has accomplished as the president of the church foreign office as well as on the council of the Evangelical Church in Germany and as church president of Hesse and Nassau cannot be finally evaluated for many years until the passion and resentment of our present church politics is removed. However, even today it is outlined with sufficient clarity to permit us to recognize the significance of a man whom a contemporary autobiography described with accuracy as the "mainspring."

The fact that such a man has been shunted about within his own church to the role of outsider and lone wolf speaks less against him than against the forces who have achieved this.

In the final analysis, while many may disagree with the tactics and methods of Germany's most controversial churchman, they cannot escape the uncomfortable fact that he speaks as God's man and as a Christian. To the questions that are plaguing the free world concerning their doubts as to coexistence with Russia, he gives not the answer of the skeptic or the cynic but of the Christian.

Does he really believe that communism and Christianity can exist side by side?

"I think communism and Christianity as ideologies are mutually exclusive," he replies. "But ideologically I cannot get along with a man who is not a Christian, who is anti-Christian, or has disowned the church. Coexistence is not a question of principle but of practice. To say that communism and Christianity cannot exist together is not to say that communists and Christians cannot exist together."

But can we trust the Russians? Will they abuse the trust?

"The moment you begin to weigh consequences," says Niemoeller, "you are lost. We talk of wanting to build a strong world. Instead, try to protect your neighbor. That makes a strong world. A world in which everyone tries to protect himself is a weak world full of envy and jealousy."

On what, then, can we base our future? What is the hope of the world? Pastor Niemoeller supplies the answer quickly, eagerly. It is the only answer that he can see.

"The hope of the world is the same as it has always been, in the beginning, in the Middle Ages, in the time of the Nazis, and today—the love of God and obedience to the beliefs and hopes and ideals of His son, Jesus Christ."

BIBLIOGRAPHY

Best, S. Payne. *The Venlo Incident.* London: Hutchinson & Co., Ltd., 1947.

Carmer, Carl. *War Against God.* New York: Henry Holt & Co., Inc., 1943.

Dibelius, Bishop Otto. *Day Is Dawning.* Philadelphia: Christian Education Press, 1956.

Frey, Dr. Arthur. *Cross and Swastika.* London: Student Christian Movement Press, 1938.

Gisevius, Hans Bernd. *To the Bitter End.* Boston: Houghton Mifflin Co., 1947.

Heiden, Konrad. *History of National Socialism.* New York: Alfred A. Knopf, Inc., 1935.

Hildebrand, Franz. *Pastor Niemoeller and His Creed.* London: Hodder & Stoughton, 1939.

Herman, Stewart. *It's Your Souls We Want.* New York: Harper & Brothers, 1943.

————. *The Rebirth of the German Church.* New York: Harper & Brothers., 1946.

Jones, Arthur S. *The Crooked Cross.* London: Macmillan War Pamphlets, 1940.

————. *The Struggle for Religious Freedom in Germany.* London: Victor Gollancz, Ltd., 1938.

Kraft, William. *Christ Versus Hitler*. New York: Lutheran Press, 1937.

Means, Paul B. *Things That Are Caesar's*. New York: Round Table Press, 1935.

Miller, Basil William. *Martin Niemoeller, Hero of the Concentration Camp*. Grand Rapids, Mich.: Zondervan Publishing House, 1942.

Niemoeller, Martin. *From U-Boat to Pulpit* (with addition by Henry Smith Leiper). Chicago: Willett, Clark & Company, 1937.

———. *Here Stand I*. Chicago: Willett, Clark & Company, 1937.

———. *The Gestapo Defied*. London: W. Hodge & Co., 1941.

———. *Dachau Sermons*. New York: Harper & Brothers, 1946.

———. *Of Guilt and Hope*. New York: Philosophical Library, Inc., 1946.

Nygren, Anders. *The Church Controversy in Germany*. London: Student Christian Movement Press, 1934.

Pinson, Koppel S. *Modern Germany, Its History and Civilization*. New York: The Macmillan Co., 1954.

Power, Michael. *Religion in the Reich*. New York: Longmans, Green & Co., Inc., 1939.

Shuster, George N. *Like a Mighty Army*. New York, London: D. Appleton-Century Co., 1935.

Stein, Leo. *I Was in Hell with Niemoeller*. New York: Fleming H. Revell Co., 1942.

Von Schuschnigg, Kurt. *Austrian Requiem*. New York: G. P. Putnam's Sons, 1946.